AMERICA ★ THE ★ BEAUTIFUL

How to Use This Book

Look for these special features in this book:

SIDEBARS, **CHARTS**, **GRAPHS**, and original **MAPS** expand your understanding of what's being discussed—and also make useful sources for classroom reports.

FAQs answer common **F**requently **A**sked **Q**uestions about people, places, and things.

WOW FACTORS offer "Who knew?" facts to keep you thinking.

TRAVEL GUIDE gives you tips on exploring the state—either in person or right from your chair!

PROJECT ROOM provides fun ideas for school assignments and incredible research projects. Plus, there's a guide to primary sources—what they are and how to cite them.

Please note: All statistics are as up-to-date as possible at the time of publication.

Consultant: Michael A. Gibson, Professor of Geology, University of Tennessee at Martin; Mary S. Hoffschwelle, Professor of History, Middle Tennessee State University; William Loren Katz

Book production by The Design Lab

Library of Congress Cataloging-in-Publication Data
Somervill, Barbara A.
 Tennessee / by Barbara A. Somervill.
    p. cm.—(America the beautiful. Third series)
 Includes bibliographical references and index.
 ISBN-13: 978-0-531-18504-9
 ISBN-10: 0-531-18504-4
 1. Tennessee—Juvenile literature. I. Title. II. Series.
 F436.3.S66 2010
 976.8—dc22   2008000505

©2010 Scholastic Inc.
All rights reserved. Published in 2010 by Children's Press, an imprint of Scholastic Inc.
Published simultaneously in Canada. Printed in the United States of America.
SCHOLASTIC, CHILDREN'S PRESS, and associated logos are trademarks and/or registered trademarks of Scholastic Inc.

1 2 3 4 5 6 7 8 9 10 R 19 18 17 16 15 14 13 12 11 10

Tennessee

BY BARBARA A. SOMERVILL

Third Series

Children's Press®
An Imprint of Scholastic Inc.
New York ★ Toronto ★ London ★ Auckland ★ Sydney
Mexico City ★ New Delhi ★ Hong Kong
Danbury, Connecticut

CONTENTS

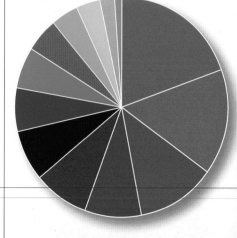

OHIO

INDIANA

WEST
VIRGINIA

ILLINOIS

KENTUCKY

World's
Largest Guitar

Bristol Motor
Speedway

MISSOURI

Tennessee National
Wildlife Refuge

Country Music Hall of
Fame and Museum

Knoxville Zoo

VIRGINIA

NASHVILLE Cumberland

Tennessee
State Capitol

Musicians Hall of
Fame and Museum

KNOXVILLE

Appalachian Mountains

NORTH
CAROLINA

TENNESSEE

Cumberland Caverns

Great Smoky Mountains
National Park

ARKANSAS

Mississippi

Tennessee

MEMPHIS

Tennessee

CHATTANOOGA

Elvis Presley's
Graceland

Sharpe
Planetarium

Creative Discovery
Museum

NASCAR
SpeedPark

SOUTH
CAROLINA

MISSISSIPPI

ALABAMA

GEORGIA

N
W E
S

0   50
Miles

MARYLAND

Welcome to Tennessee!

HOW DID TENNESSEE GET ITS NAME?

The word *Tennessee* comes from Tanasi, the name of the principal town of the Overhill Cherokee people. No one is certain what the word *tanasi* actually means. Some historians think that it might have meant "river with a big bend." When Europeans first arrived in the area, the main river was also named *Tanasi*. That river is now called the Tennessee.

TENNESSEE

ATLANTIC
OCEAN

8

READ ABOUT

Fall color in Great
Smoky Mountains
National Park

CHAPTER ONE

LAND

⋆

THE GREAT SMOKY MOUNTAINS, IN THE SOUTHEASTERN UNITED STATES, MARK TENNESSEE'S EAST-ERN BORDER. The mighty Mississippi River defines the western border. Between the two borders lie rolling hills, flat tablelands, and long river valleys. Tennessee is a fairly small state, measuring 42,143 square miles (109,150 square kilometers). The highest point is Clingmans Dome at 6,643 feet (2,025 meters), located in the Great Smoky Mountains of Sevier County. The lowest point lies along the Mississippi River at 178 feet (54 m).

Tennessee's Topography

Use the color-coded elevation chart to see on the map Tennessee's high points (dark red to orange) and low points (green to dark green). Elevation is measured as the distance above or below sea level.

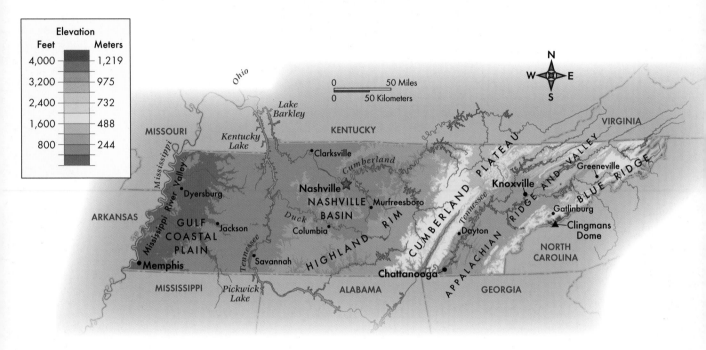

ASSEMBLING TENNESSEE

Beginning 800 million years ago, oceans covered Tennessee several times. When creatures and plants died, their remains fell to the seafloor. Layers of sand and silt also built up on the seafloor. Over millions of years, pressure from the water and layers above changed this material into deep layers of **sedimentary** rock such as limestone, shale, and sandstone. Hidden in the layers of stone are fossils of ancient sea creatures such as plesiosaurs, which looked like long-necked dinosaurs with flippers. The Tennessee state fossil, *Pterotrigonia thoracica,* is a fossilized marine clam that lived in the

WORD TO KNOW

sedimentary *formed from clay, sand, and gravel that settle at the bottom of a body of water*

oceans of western Tennessee 72 million years ago. The last of the oceans retreated from Tennessee about 65 million years ago, and Tennessee became a land environment.

Other forces also built Tennessee. Between 310 million and 245 million years ago, giant pieces of Earth's crust moved underneath the area that is now eastern Tennessee. As these pieces pushed against one another, the land crumpled, rose, and formed the Blue Ridge and Great Smoky mountains. They are among the oldest mountains in North America.

Underground water seeped through and eroded the limestone in Tennessee, creating many caves. In 1998,

Scientists have discovered information about Tennessee's past at dig sites like this one at Shiloh National Military Park.

Tennessee Geo-Facts

Along with the state's geographical highlights, this chart ranks Tennessee's land, water, and total area compared to all other states.

Total area; rank . . . . . 42,143 square miles (109,150 sq km); 36th
Land; rank . . . . 41,217 square miles (106,752 sq km); 34th
Water; rank . . . . 926 square miles (2,398 sq km); 32nd
Inland water; rank . . . . 926 square miles (2,398 sq km); 24th
Geographic center . . . . Rutherford County, 5 miles (8 km) northeast of Murfreesboro
Latitude . . . . 35° N to 36°41' N
Longitude . . . . 81°37' W to 90°28' W
Highest point . . . . Clingmans Dome, 6,643 feet (2,025 m), in Sevier County
Lowest point . . . Mississippi River in Shelby County, 178 feet (54 m)
Largest city . . . . Memphis
Longest river . . . . Tennessee

Source: U.S. Census Bureau

WOW Rhode Island, the smallest state, could fit inside Tennessee 27 times, and Tennessee could fit inside Alaska, the largest state, almost 16 times.

SEE IT HERE!

UNDERGROUND TENNESSEE

Over thousands of years, groundwater seeped up through pores and cracks in the rocks, eventually carving dramatic caverns beneath the land of Tennessee. The state is riddled with caves, some bearing unusual names such as Big Bone Cave, Waterfall Plunge, and Snail Shell Cave. Blue Spring Cave is the longest at 33 miles (53 km). The deepest cave is Bull Cave, lying 924 feet (282 m) below the earth. Cumberland Caverns attracts the most tourists.

WORD TO KNOW

geographers *people who study and describe the earth's surface*

hydrocarbons *chemical compounds made of hydrogen and carbon*

explorers mapping Rumbling Falls Cave stumbled onto the largest single cave room in the eastern United States, now called the Rumble Room. The state's many caves, waterfalls, rushing rivers, and sheer cliffs cut the landscape and create stunningly beautiful scenery.

LAND REGIONS

Tennesseans divide their state into three "grand divisions": East Tennessee, Middle Tennessee, and West Tennessee, but **geographers** divide the state into six major regions based on the landscape. Those regions, from east to west, are the Blue Ridge, the Appalachian Ridge and Valley, the Cumberland Plateau, the Highland Rim, the Nashville Basin, and the Gulf Coastal Plain.

Blue Ridge Region

The Blue Ridge region, which runs along the border with North Carolina, includes several mountain ranges, including the Great Smoky Mountains, the Unicoi Range, the Iron Mountains, the Crab Orchard Mountains, the Cumberland Mountains, and the Blue Ridge Mountains. Tennessee's mountains, which are part of the larger Appalachian Mountain range, are old and eroded, so the peaks are not very high. Clingmans Dome, the highest point in the state, lies in the Great Smokies.

The Blue Ridge Mountains earned their name because, from a distance, they appear a rich, lush blue. Trees in these mountains give off **hydrocarbons** that make the bluish color. The rugged Blue Ridge landscape includes heavily forested slopes, steep gorges, and rushing rivers and streams.

The Great Smoky Mountains get their name from a natural haze that fills the valleys, making the mountains look as though they are blanketed in smoke.

The Blue Ridge Mountains have a rich blue color when viewed from a distance.

A hiker takes a break on the Appalachian Trail, which runs through Great Smoky Mountains National Park.

Appalachian Ridge and Valley

The Appalachian Ridge and Valley region lies to the west of the Blue Ridge region. The ridge and valley consists of long, parallel valleys separated by forested ridges. The dominant feature in this region is the Tennessee River.

Cumberland Plateau

Directly west of the Appalachian Ridge and Valley lies the Cumberland Plateau. This high tableland, which ranges from 1,500 to 1,800 feet (457 to 550 m) above sea level, is covered with flat-topped mountains and steep valleys. An almost perfectly straight valley called Sequatchie Valley slices through the Cumberland Plateau for 150 miles (240 km) in Tennessee and Alabama.

Highland Rim and Nashville Basin Regions

West of the Cumberland Plateau, the Highland Rim surrounds the low-lying Nashville Basin. The Highland

Rim is younger geologically, while **erosion** has worn down the Nashville Basin, exposing older rock. Both regions have many farms.

Gulf Coastal Plain

The land between the Mississippi River and the western section of the Tennessee River is called the Gulf Coastal Plain. This region stretches all the way from the Gulf of Mexico to southern Illinois and is the largest land region in Tennessee. The western part of the Gulf Coastal Plain is a lowland less than 300 feet (90 m) above sea level, called the Tennessee Bottoms.

Rivers and Lakes

Two rivers dominate the Tennessee landscape: the Mississippi and the Tennessee. Wetlands near the broad, winding Mississippi River are home to diverse wildlife, including otters, owls, and ospreys. The Hatchie River, a small **tributary** of the Mississippi, is home to 11 species of catfish, more than any other North American river.

The Tennessee River begins where the Holston and French Broad rivers meet near Knoxville in East Tennessee. The river winds its way south, dipping into Alabama before heading west into Mississippi and then north again through Tennessee and into Kentucky. The Tennessee's many tributaries include the Duck and the Big Sandy. Several of the Tennessee's lesser tributaries—including the Nantahala, the Ocoee, the Pigeon, and the Chattooga—are popular for kayaking, canoeing, and whitewater rafting.

WORDS TO KNOW

erosion *the gradual wearing away of rock or soil by physical breakdown, chemical solution, or water*

tributary *a smaller river that flows into a larger river*

Rafting on the Ocoee River

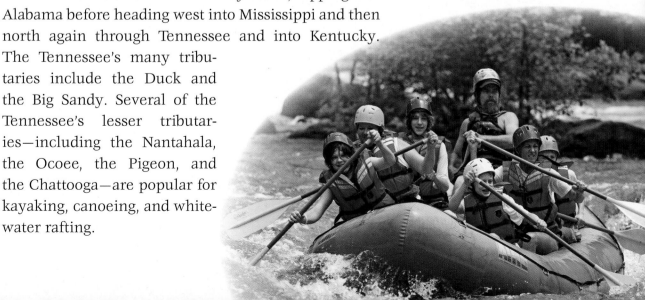

The Tennessee River was once wild and frequently flooded its banks. Today, a series of dams on the river prevent flooding, create electric power, and manage the freshwater supply throughout East and Middle Tennessee.

Damming rivers created most of Tennessee's more than 1,000 lakes. The state's largest natural lake is Reelfoot Lake, which was formed by earthquakes in 1811 and 1812. The earthquakes shifted sediment layers under a section of the Mississippi River, creating a natural dam that blocked some water, forming Reelfoot Lake. Kentucky Lake, on the Tennessee–Kentucky border, is one of the largest **reservoirs** in the United States. It measures 184 miles (296 km) long and has more than 2,000 miles (3,220 km) of shoreline.

WORD TO KNOW

reservoirs *artificial lakes or tanks created for water storage*

Cypress trees in Reelfoot Lake

CLIMATE

The warmest section of Tennessee is the west. This region has mild temperatures and high humidity. Memphis, the largest city in West Tennessee, has an average daily high temperature of 49°F (9°C) in January and 92°F (33°C) in July. Nashville, in the central region, is slightly cooler. In the mountains, winters are much colder, with snow and occasional ice storms. Summers are cool, with temperatures generally 5 to 10 degrees F (3 to 6 degrees C) cooler than in Memphis.

AL GORE: NOBEL PEACE PRIZE WINNER

Al Gore (1948–) has enjoyed two impressive careers: he has been a politician and an environmental activist. As a politician, he represented Tennessee in the U.S. House of Representatives and Senate, served as vice president of the United States from 1993 to 2001, and nearly won the presidency in 2000. As an environmental activist, he has increased awareness about **global warming**. In 2006, he starred in a documentary about global warming called An Inconvenient Truth. For his environmental work, Gore shared the 2007 Nobel Peace Prize with the Intergovernmental Panel on Climate Change, a scientific group established by two United Nations organizations.

? Want to know more? See www.biography.com/search/article.do?id=9316028

Weather Report

This chart shows record temperatures (high and low) for the state, as well as average temperatures (July and January) and average annual precipitation.

Record high temperature . . . . 113°F (45°C) at Perryville
on July 29 and August 9, 1930
Record low temperature . . . . –32°F (–36°C) at Mountain City
on December 30, 1917
Average July temperature . . . . 79°F (26°C)
Average January temperature . . . . 37°F (3°C)
Average annual precipitation . . . . 48 inches (122 cm)

Source: National Climatic Data Center, NESDIS, NOAA, U.S. Department of Commerce

WORD TO KNOW

global warming *an increase in temperatures around the globe, particularly as a result of pollution*

Dogwoods in bloom in the Great Smoky Mountains

WORD TO KNOW

precipitation *all water that falls to the earth, including rain, sleet, hail, snow, dew, fog, or mist*

FAQ ★ ★ ★

Q8 WHAT WAS THE HEAVI-EST SNOWFALL RECORDED IN TENNESSEE HISTORY?

A8 In March 1993, a storm dumped more than 4.5 feet (1.4 m) of snow in one day on LeComte, Tennessee.

The rainiest time of the year is early spring, with the greatest rainfall in March. September and October tend to be dry and mild throughout the state. The state as a whole receives an average of 48 inches (122 cm) of **precipitation** per year. Snowfall ranges from 5 inches (13 cm) in West Tennessee to 16 inches (41 cm) in the eastern mountains.

PLANT LIFE

Imagine springtime in Tennessee. In the mountains, lacy white dogwoods bloom near clusters of rosy pink rhododendrons and the pale pink blossoms of eastern rosebud. Bigleaf magnolia, a common evergreen tree, brightens the woods with large cream-colored blooms. Forest landscapes include every possible shade of green, as leaves burst out on hickory, hop hornbeam, slippery elm, hackberry, and beech trees.

Forest meadows and road-sides come alive with wild-flowers during the spring and summer months. Bright black-eyed Susans, honeysuckles, and tall goldenrods sprinkle the woods with sunny shades of yellow. Red and white clovers add to the color, along with pink, purple, and blue-white morning glories.

The dense green vine that appears to be swallow-ing up other plants is kudzu. Originally brought from Japan to feed cattle and control soil erosion, this plant strangles shrubs and trees native to the region and is changing the landscape of Tennessee.

Black-eyed Susans

ENDANGERED SPECIES

Tennessee has 90 **endangered** and **threatened** species. Plants on the list include Blue Ridge goldenrod, Eggert's sunflower, leafy prairie clover, and American hart's-tongue fern. Green blossoms and yellow blossoms may sound like flowers, but they are actually endangered mussel species. Other endangered animals include the Indiana and gray bats, the eastern puma, the Carolina northern flying squirrel, and the least tern. The Tennessee Department of Environment and Conservation is working to preserve the habitats of these creatures so they can survive.

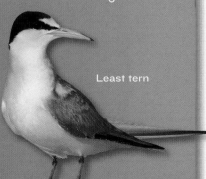

Least tern

WORDS TO KNOW

endangered *at risk of becoming extinct throughout all or part of its range*

threatened *likely to become endangered in the foreseeable future*

One of Tennessee's most endangered plants is a predator. Insects crawl inside the green pitcher plant, which dissolves the captured insects' bodies and uses them for nutrition.

Black bears make their home in the mountains of Tennessee.

In the swampy wetlands of southwestern Tennessee, loblolly pines, cypress, and gum trees sway in warm spring breezes. Reeds and water lilies sprout along the water's edge.

ANIMAL LIFE

Tennessee's forests are alive with small mammals such as raccoons, opossums, rabbits, and squirrels. The state also boasts healthy populations of larger mammals, including black bears, white-tailed deer, and elk. The mountains of Tennessee are home to mountain lions. These predators were hunted relentlessly in the past, but they still survive in remote areas.

Plenty of forestland means plenty of birds. Golden and bald eagles, ospreys, and hawks swoop through the sky, searching for fish, birds, or rodents. Cardinals,

bluebirds, and Carolina wrens twitter from the pines and oaks, while egrets, blue herons, and cranes dip their heads to feed in wetland waters.

Tennessee waters are alive with catfish, smallmouth bass, bluegills, and darters. Mussels bearing colorful names such as washboard mussels, ebonyshells, and pink heelsplitters abound.

The endangered southern cavefish has an eerie white color and no eyes. These small fish live in the pitch-black darkness of Tennessee's underground rivers and pools.

Tennessee National Park Areas

This map shows some of Tennessee's national parks, monuments, preserves, and other areas protected by the National Park Service.

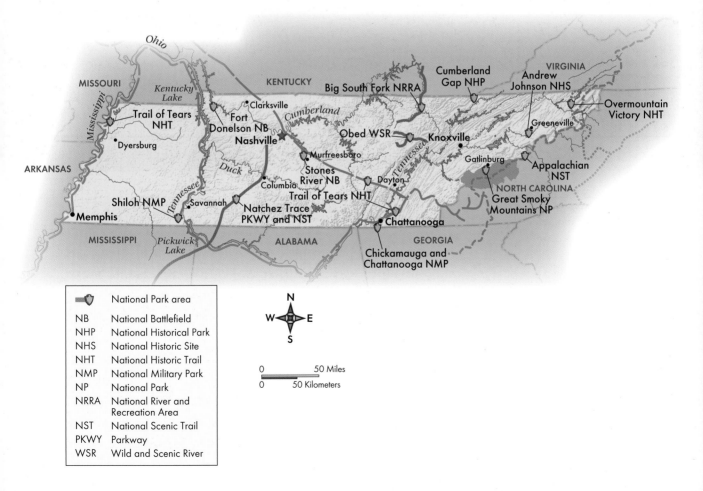

🛡	National Park area
NB	National Battlefield
NHP	National Historical Park
NHS	National Historic Site
NHT	National Historic Trail
NMP	National Military Park
NP	National Park
NRRA	National River and Recreation Area
NST	National Scenic Trail
PKWY	Parkway
WSR	Wild and Scenic River

Factories, such as this coal-fired power plant in Kingston, can pollute Tennessee's water and air.

PROTECTING THE ENVIRONMENT

Among the most pressing environmental issues facing Tennessee is maintaining clean water and clean air. Rainwater carries fertilizers, pesticides, animal waste, oil, and other pollutants from farms and factories to streams and rivers. As a result, the state's freshwater sources have a range of pollution.

In 2000, the state issued warnings about swimming in more than 110 miles (177 km) of river because of water pollution. Many lakes and streams were so polluted that they could not support fish, snails, clams, or other life. Two years later, the state formed the Clean

Water Challenge. As part of this effort, the state educates Tennesseans about how pollutants from fertilizers to battery acid to household cleaning products get from their lawns and driveways into the water supply. The state is also working with businesses and farms to control pollution.

Tennessee's air pollution is caused by both industry and heavy car use. The state hopes to decrease air pollution by encouraging people to take trains or buses or drive in carpools. State employees get a bonus for carpooling or using public transportation. The state also allows some government employees to work out of their homes so they reduce car trips. In these and many other ways, Tennesseans are doing their part to keep their state livable.

THINK ABOUT IT!

Pollution in the Park

Great Smoky Mountains National Park has the worst air pollution of any national park in the country. This pollution comes from industry, automobiles, and power plants that burn coal. Some people want power companies to be able to build even more coal-burning power plants in the region. Many others think this is a bad idea. Iliff McMahon Jr., mayor of Cocke County, which borders the park, has pointed out, "Poor air quality affects the experiences and health of summer visitors, which affects our economy. It doesn't make sense . . . to encourage more polluting coal-fired power plants to build in the Smokies' backyard. Especially when we are already doing everything possible to improve our air quality."

READ ABOUT

Archaic people
preparing food
over fires

Woodland
water bottle

c. 15,000 BCE

*The first people arrive in
what is now Tennessee*

c. 8000 BCE

*The Archaic Period
begins*

▲ **c. 300 BCE**

*Woodland culture
develops*

CHAPTER TWO

FIRST PEOPLE

★

HUMANS MAY HAVE ARRIVED IN WHAT IS NOW TENNESSEE AS EARLY AS 17,000 YEARS AGO. Their ancestors probably crossed from present-day Russia to Alaska at a time when the water between them was frozen. They may also have crossed in boats. Over several thousand years, humans moved south, spreading over North America and eventually into today's Tennessee. Scientists call these people Paleo-Indians.

c. 900 CE

Mississippian culture emerges

c. 1400s ▶

Chickasaws, Cherokees, and other Native American nations develop

Cherokee basket

1500s

Shawnees move into Tennessee

Paleo-Indians hunted mastodons and other big game animals.

In some Tennessee caves, scientists have found prints of human feet in hardened mud or clay. Some of these footprints date back more than 4,000 years.

PEOPLE ARRIVE

Paleo-Indians lived in communities of 50 to 150 people. Caves or temporary shelters served as housing. Women raised the children; butchered game; made clothing and household goods; collected roots, berries, fruit, and nuts; and maintained the group's most precious possession—fire. Fire kept people warm, protected them from animal attacks, and cooked their food. Men did most of the hunting. Paleo-Indians hunted mastodons, mammoths, giant sloths, and massive beavers for their meat, fur, and bones. They used every part of the animals.

ARCHAIC PEOPLE

Around 8000 BCE, the large game animals died off, and people had to find other ways to get food. This was the beginning of the Archaic Period. Archaic people began hunting smaller animals such as deer. They also collected shellfish. Agriculture started during the Archaic Period. People began growing squash and sunflowers rather than just gathering what fruit and seeds they found.

THE WOODLAND PERIOD

The Archaic Period was followed by the Woodland Period, which stretched from about 300 BCE to 900 CE. During the Woodland Period, people's diets became more varied as they grew grapes, beans, corn, and other foods. They wove baskets and developed pottery, which they decorated with abstract designs, birds, or snakes. Woodland people created jewelry from copper, stones, and carved wood. They also strung freshwater pearls to make bracelets and necklaces. Some Woodland peoples began building large mounds of earth in which they buried their dead.

Water bottle from the Woodland Period

MISSISSIPPIAN CULTURE

Between 900 and 1450, the Mississippian culture emerged from the Woodland culture. The Mississippians were Mound Builders. They built large, flat-topped mounds in the shape of stunted pyramids. They continued to use the mounds as burial grounds, but they also built religious temples atop them. Some nobles lived in homes built on the mounds.

In Tennessee, Mississippians built a city now called Mound Bottom on the Harpeth River. Mound Bottom served as a religious, agricultural, and trade center, and the region surrounding it was home to thousands of

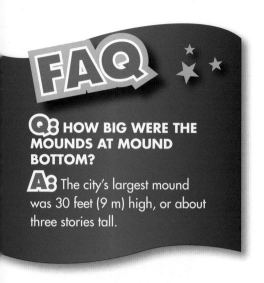

FAQ

Q8 HOW BIG WERE THE MOUNDS AT MOUND BOTTOM?

A8 The city's largest mound was 30 feet (9 m) high, or about three stories tall.

people. Mississippians built high wooden barricades that protected their homes, warehouses, and community buildings in Mound Bottom.

NATIVE AMERICAN NATIONS

In the late 1400s, the Mississippian culture entered a period of change. Warfare increased, and many people moved. Slowly, the Mississippian culture disappeared, and dozens of new groups took its place. Native American nations that developed in Tennessee include Chickasaws, Cherokees, Yuchis, and Creeks,

A Mississippian village

Native American Peoples
(Before European Contact)

This map shows the general area of Native American peoples before European settlers arrived.

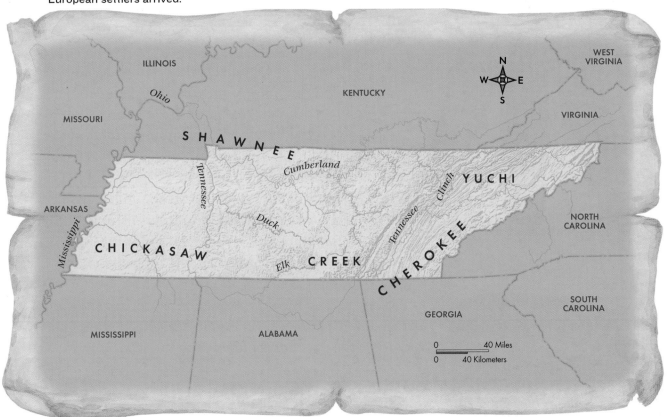

with the Chickasaws and the Cherokees being the largest groups. Another group, the Shawnees, moved south into Tennessee in the 1500s and 1600s.

All of these people survived by fishing, hunting, and farming. They depended heavily on growing corn, beans, and squash, which were known as the Three Sisters. One main advantage of the Three Sisters was that they could be grown in the same field. Corn grew

Corn was one of the main crops for Native Americans.

on stalks up to 7 feet (2 m) high. The stalks could support pole beans, which nourished the soil. Squash grew along the ground, with broad leaves to protect the soil from wind and hold in moisture. Native people ate the three crops fresh or dried them for use months later.

Different groups of Native Americans in Tennessee had similar attitudes toward family life and the roles of men and women. Women managed family life, home life, and agriculture. They owned their homes, although men probably built the dwellings. When a woman married, her husband moved in with her family.

Men were responsible for life outside the home, including hunting, fishing, and relationships with other communities. Men participated in political and religious events, whereas women usually did not. When a Native American nation went to war, men were expected to fight. Some Cherokee women also fought in wars, but they were the exception rather than the rule.

CHICKASAWS

Chickasaws occupied territory from the Mississippi River to the western Tennessee River and south into what is now Mississippi. They lived in small villages headed by local chiefs and councils.

Chickasaw women traditionally wore dresses made from animal hides. During winter months, women kept warm by wrapping up in bison calf skins. They made moccasins from deer, bear, or elk skin that had been carefully tanned to keep the leather soft. Many hours were spent decorating moccasins with shells and beads.

FAQ ★ ★ ★

Q8 WHAT GAME DID CHICKASAWS PLAY ON THEIR BALL FIELDS?

A8 They played a game called *toli*, which was much like modern-day lacrosse. The field was 500 feet (152 m) long, with a goal at each end. Players carried sticks with a net attached to the end. Teammates passed a ball to one another, catching it with the net. Their object was to reach the end of the field and throw the ball into the goal. Play was rough—cuts and bruises were part of the game.

Many Native American groups played a game that is similar to today's lacrosse.

In the summer, men wore **breechcloths** and shirts. Their winter garments included skins from mountain lions, beavers, and bears. These wraps were worn with the fur on the inside for added warmth. Men wore their hair long but shaved the sides of their heads.

Chickasaw villages consisted of several households. A household kept a summer house and a winter house, as well as a storage building for dried corn and other dried vegetables. The village also included a council house, a ball field, and a place for religious ceremonies.

CHEROKEES

Cherokees lived in what is now East Tennessee, where they built towns such as Chota, Tanasi, Toqua, Tuskegee, and Tallassee. Cherokees were divided into seven clans, groups of people made up of smaller families. Clan membership passed down through the mother, and a

WORD TO KNOW

breechcloths *garments worn by men over their lower bodies*

Picture Yourself . . .

Preparing for the Green Corn Ceremony

It is late summer, time for the Green Corn Ceremony. You and your sisters have been tending fields for months, and now the corn is ripe enough to eat. Young men from town travel to neighboring villages to announce the day when the Green Corn Ceremony will be held. The messengers gather seven ears of corn, one ear each from the field of a different clan. While the messengers are away, the town leader and seven councillors **fast** for six days. On the seventh day, the ceremony begins, and the fast is broken. On this day, a sacred fire is put out and a new fire is started. You celebrate with your family and friends, hoping for a good harvest that will feed everyone throughout the year.

WORD TO KNOW

fast *to go without eating*

man moved in with his wife's household when they married.

Cherokee villages had populations of 100 to 400 people. Every village had a central plaza and a central council house that was used for public meetings, religious ceremonies, and planning wars. Around the central plaza, Cherokees built their homes. Families built a circular winter house and a rectangular summer house. Houses were made of mud and sticks with reeds serving as roofing. Most houses had holes in the center of the roof to let smoke from the fire escape. Beyond the central plaza, Cherokees planted fields of corn, beans, squash, cabbage, melons, and peas. Some villages also maintained fruit trees.

The Cherokees believed in colors as symbols of spirits and life. Red was the color of the east and represented success and triumph in battle. Blue was the

Cherokee basket

A number of Native American groups celebrated a good harvest with the Green Corn Ceremony and other rituals.

color of the north, a symbol of failure and trouble. Black came on the west wind and represented death. From the south came white, which stood for peace and happiness. Cherokees used these symbolic colors in religion, war, and personal life. Red beads on a person's clothing aided recovery from sickness. In battle, Cherokee warriors attacked their enemies with black war clubs. People ate white food or walked on a white trail to a white dwelling in search of happiness.

For the most part, Cherokees lived happily in their land called Tanasi. They could not foresee the changes that they would face once Europeans crossed their land.

READ ABOUT

Spanish explorer
Hernando de
Soto at the
Mississippi River

1540

*Spaniard Hernando
de Soto leads the first
European expedition
into Tennessee*

1673 ►

*Jacques Marquette
(above) and Louis Joliet
are the first French to
arrive in Tennessee*

1673

*The British begin
exploring the
Tennessee region*

CHAPTER THREE

EXPLORATION AND SETTLEMENT

★

MOST EUROPEANS WHO CAME TO THE REGION WERE IN SEARCH OF GOLD. Hernando de Soto and his troops arrived from Spain in 1540. When they arrived in Chiaha, the local people provided them with food and shelter. But de Soto's group was cruel and forced the Native people to work. In another town, the Spaniards stole food and other goods and took a leader hostage to obtain guides. The Native people were relieved to see the de Soto party leave.

1763
Great Britain gains lands east of the Mississippi, including Tennessee

1772
British settlers create an independent government called the Watauga Association

1783 ▸
The American Revolution ends, and Tennessee is part of a new nation

European Exploration of Tennessee

The colored arrows on this map show the routes taken by explorers between 1539 and 1682.

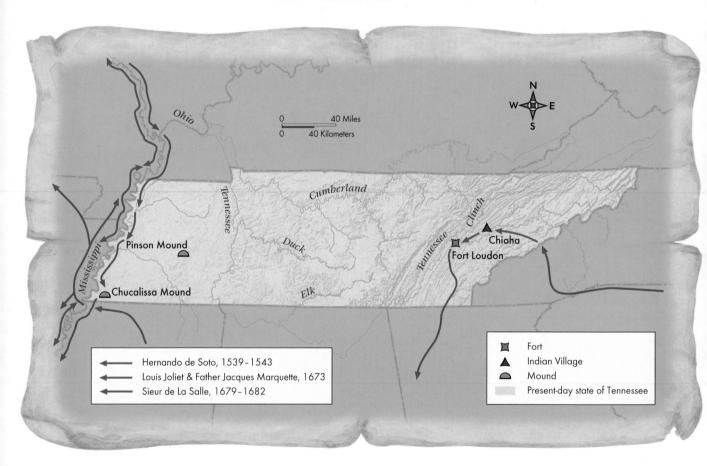

Hernando de Soto, 1539–1543
Louis Joliet & Father Jacques Marquette, 1673
Sieur de La Salle, 1679–1682

Fort
Indian Village
Mound
Present-day state of Tennessee

SPANISH EXPEDITIONS

Twenty years after Hernando de Soto traveled through Tennessee, a second Spanish **expedition** arrived near what is now Chattanooga. This expedition, headed by Tristán de Luna y Arellano, was searching for a route to the Coosa Nation, a Native group in what is now northern Georgia. Luna's men clashed with some Native people along the Tennessee River and eventually left.

Many Native Americans died from diseases brought by explorers who traveled through their land.

A Spanish expedition under Juan Pardo explored some areas of Tennessee in 1566–1567. He had several forts built and, like most Spanish explorers, hoped to find gold.

None of the early Spanish expeditions were successful. They found no gold, gems, or other great wealth. They treated Native people with cruelty, creating bitter enemies.

The Spanish also carried common European diseases that were new to the Native people. Thousands of Native men, women, and children died from smallpox,

WORD TO KNOW

expedition *a trip for the purpose of exploration*

measles, chicken pox, and whooping cough, because their bodies had never before been exposed to the diseases and had no natural **immunity** against them.

THE FRENCH AND ENGLISH ARRIVE

Just over 100 years later, in 1673, the French arrived in Tennessee. Father Jacques Marquette, a **missionary**, and Louis Joliet, a fur trader, led an expedition down the Mississippi River from Illinois to the Gulf of Mexico. Along the way, the French stopped at Chickasaw Bluffs near today's Memphis. Unlike the Spanish, the French wanted to get along with the Native people so they could trade with them. The Chickasaw people, however, did not want to deal with the French and prevented them from establishing control over the Mississippi River in the Tennessee region.

A second French expedition, led by René-Robert Cavelier, Sieur de La Salle, built a fort near the mouth of the Hatchie River in southwestern Tennessee. La

WORD TO KNOW

immunity *a body's defense against disease*

missionary *a person who tries to convert others to a religion*

Jacques Marquette (standing), Louis Joliet (back of boat), and their guides on the Mississippi River, 1673

Salle paved the way for the French to extend their trading network up the Mississippi and inland along Tennessee's major rivers. The French provided Native groups with iron goods, guns and ammunition, cloth, blankets, and food in exchange for furs. Fur trading made the French wealthy. The French trading post at French Lick was at the site of present-day Nashville.

Meanwhile, the English had started colonies along the Atlantic Coast. They wanted to gain more land and to increase trade. English explorations of Tennessee began when Abraham Wood, a Virginia merchant, sent James Needham and Gabriel Arthur to establish trade with the Cherokee people. Needham and Arthur arrived in Cherokee territory in 1673, the same year that Marquette and Joliet sailed down the Mississippi. Needham was killed on the trip, but Arthur returned to Virginia a year later, having made friends with the Cherokees. Over the next decades, more English entered Tennessee, first to set up trading posts and then to build settlements.

In 1749, Dr. Thomas Walker of the Loyal Land Company explored Tennessee to claim lands for British settlers. With both the French and British expanding into Kentucky, Tennessee, and Ohio, it was only a matter of time before the two old rivals clashed.

MINI-BIO

ATTAKULLAKULLA: CHEROKEE LEADER

Cherokee leader Attakullakulla (1700–1780) helped solidify the relationship between the Cherokee people and the British colonial governments of South Carolina and Virginia. In 1730, he and six other Cherokees accompanied Sir Alexander Cumming to England to meet with officials there. When American Revolutionary troops occupied Cherokee land in 1776, Attakullakulla arranged for their withdrawal. He worked toward peaceful relations between Cherokees and settlers. As he aged, his influence among Cherokees lessened, and younger Cherokees battled the invading white settlers.

❓ **Want to know more?** See http://tennesseeencyclopedia.net/imagegallery.php?EntryID=A045

FAQ ★ ★ ★

Q8 WHAT ARE OVERMOUNTAIN MEN?

A8 The first British people to settle in Tennessee were sometimes called Overmountain Men because they were the first to settle the western side of—or "over"—the Appalachian Mountains.

THE EFFECTS OF A DISTANT WAR

In 1754, the French and British went to war over control of North America and its fur trade. During the French and Indian War, some Native Americans fought on the side of the French. Cherokees, however, sided with the British. At the war's end in 1763, France gave up Tennessee and all other French land east of the Mississippi.

Although the British government ordered all colonial settlements to remain east of the Appalachian Mountains, a few pioneers trekked into the rugged mountains of East Tennessee. William Bean of Virginia was one of the earliest British settlers in Tennessee. Bean and his wife arrived in 1769 and built a house along Boones Creek. A couple of years later, James Robertson and a group of North Carolinians joined the Beans to form a small community along the Watauga River. Small towns also sprang up in Carters Valley, Nolichucky, and Holston.

White settlers wanted good land with easy access to freshwater, but Native Americans already occupied

Settlers outside a cabin in Rugby

this land. The newcomers started pushing Native Americans off their lands. They made treaties with the Natives, which they later broke.

A thriving community of about 70 farms grew along the Watauga River. The newcomers to this area lived deep in Cherokee territory, beyond the reach of the British government. In 1772, the settlers wrote a constitution that basically followed the Virginia code of laws and outlined the organization of a typical county government of that time. Watauga citizens elected five magistrates who formed a court and ran the government. The magistrates served as governors, lawmakers, and judges. The Watauga Association, as it was called, was its own independent government.

In 1775, 13 British colonies along the East Coast began fighting for their independence from Great Britain. Little fighting took place in Tennessee during the American Revolution, but by the time the war ended in 1783, Tennessee was under the control of a new nation: the United States of America.

MINI-BIO

DAVID CROCKETT: TENNESSEE PIONEER

Born in 1786 in the mountains of East Tennessee, David "Davy" Crockett (1786–1836) became a legendary pioneer, hunter, explorer, and politician. When the War of 1812 began, Crockett volunteered for the army. He later served several terms in the U.S. House of Representatives and then went to Texas to help the fight for independence there. He died defending the Alamo from the Mexican army in 1836 and became a folk hero.

 Want to know more? See www.tshaonline. org/handbook/online/articles/CC/fcr24.html

THE STATE OF FRANKLIN

At the end of the American Revolution, the Tennessee region was claimed by North Carolina. Acting on the belief that the Cherokees lost their land because they sided with the British during the Revolution, North Carolina sold large tracts of Tennessee land to potential settlers.

Wealthy men in North Carolina quickly claimed more than 4 million acres (1.6 million hectares) of western lands. These men then decided to break from North Carolina and establish a new state called Franklin. Revolutionary War hero John Sevier, who would later become the first governor of Tennessee, was elected governor of Franklin. But Congress would not accept Franklin as a new state, and by 1790, the region was once again part of North Carolina.

The first page of Tennessee's constitution, 1796

We the People of the St...
of the United States South of the Ri...
Ohio having the right of admission into...
General Government as a member State...
consistent with the Constitution of the U...
States and the act of Cession of the Stat...
North Carolina recognizing the Ordina...
for the Government of the Territory of the...
States Northwest of the River Ohio,...
and establish the following Constitution o...
of Government and do mutually agree w...
each other to form ourselves into a free a...
...dant State by the name of the S...

1796 ▸
Tennessee becomes the 16th state

1813
Tennessee militia and Creeks clash in the Creek War

1838
Cherokees are forced west on the Trail of Tears

CHAPTER FOUR

GROWTH AND CHANGE

★

I N 1790, TENNESSEE BECAME PART OF THE SOUTHWEST TERRITORY. To become a state, Tennessee needed a population of 60,000. It also needed a constitution, so in January 1796, delegates gathered in Knoxville to begin writing one. In June 1796, President George Washington signed documents admitting Tennessee as the 16th state.

1861 ▶

The Civil War begins and Tennessee joins the Confederacy

1866

Tennessee is readmitted to the Union

late 1800s

Tennessee enacts Jim Crow laws, establishing legal segregation

Tennessee: From Territory to Statehood
(1790–1796)

This map shows the original Southwest Territory and the area (in yellow) that became the state of Tennessee in 1796.

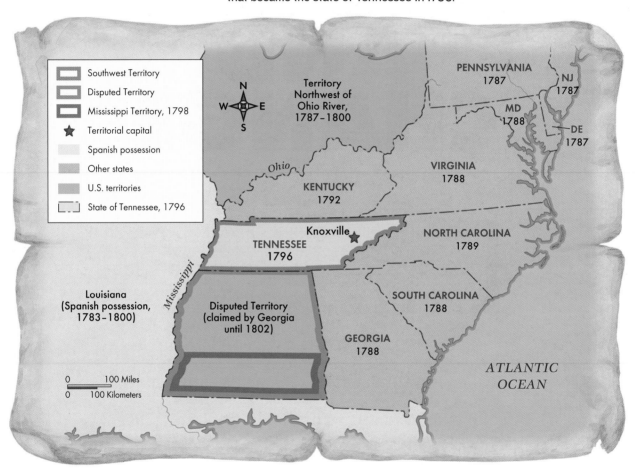

Legend:
- Southwest Territory
- Disputed Territory
- Mississippi Territory, 1798
- ★ Territorial capital
- Spanish possession
- Other states
- U.S. territories
- State of Tennessee, 1796

PENNSYLVANIA 1787

NJ 1787

MD 1788

DE 1787

Territory Northwest of Ohio River, 1787–1800

VIRGINIA 1788

Ohio

KENTUCKY 1792

Knoxville ★

TENNESSEE 1796

NORTH CAROLINA 1789

Louisiana (Spanish possession, 1783–1800)

Mississippi

Disputed Territory (claimed by Georgia until 1802)

SOUTH CAROLINA 1788

GEORGIA 1788

ATLANTIC OCEAN

0   100 Miles
0   100 Kilometers

THE WAR OF 1812

British ships stopped American vessels at sea, captured sailors, and forced them to work for the British navy, in a practice called impressment. At the time, Great Britain was also at war with France, and the British did not want the United States trading with France. Sixteen years after

Tennessee became a state, the United States entered the War of 1812 against Great Britain over these issues.

To help ensure victory in the war, Great Britain encouraged the Creeks to attack settlers along the frontier, including in Tennessee. Shawnee leader Tecumseh was also trying to unite Native Americans to fight American settlement. He recruited Creeks as part of this effort. On August 30, 1813, Creeks attacked white settlers and other Native Americans at Fort Mims near what is now Mobile, Alabama. This was part of

FAQ

Q: WHY IS TENNESSEE CALLED THE VOLUNTEER STATE?

A: Some say it's because during the War of 1812, volunteer soldiers from Tennessee played a major role in winning the war. Others argue that the name came from the large numbers of Tennesseans who volunteered to serve in the Mexican American War of 1848.

During the War of 1812, Andrew Jackson led troops from the U.S. Army against the Creek forces.

Picture Yourself . . .

Getting Sick in the Tennessee Wilderness
Your farm is on the edge of the wilderness. When your sister gets sick, you immediately turn to *Gunn's Domestic Medicine*, which was published in Knoxville in 1830. The book covers every possible ailment, from baby rashes to measles to warts. Today, you must deal with threadworms, small worms that can live inside you. According to the book, calomel, wormseed oil, and Carolina pink root fix the problem. Following the book's directions, you prepare a tea of pink root and honey and give it to your sister. For you and your family, *Gunn's* is the only link to medical care.

WORDS TO KNOW

militia *an army made up of citizens trained to serve as soldiers in an emergency*

Creoles *people of French ancestry who lived in the southern United States and spoke a version of French*

the Creek War, which became linked to the War of 1812. During the war, Tennessee's Andrew Jackson served as a major general in the U.S. Army. He and his forces, including 3,500 troops from Tennessee, defeated the Creeks. In August 1814, Jackson forced the Creeks to agree to a treaty giving up nearly two-thirds of their land.

Following his efforts in the Creek War, Jackson led troops into battle in New Orleans, Louisiana. Jackson's army consisted of a **militia** from Tennessee and Kentucky, regular U.S. Army soldiers, Choctaws, free African Americans, **Creoles**, and pirates. This ragtag group went into battle against Britain's elite troops, defeating them at the Battle of New Orleans on January 8, 1815. This victory made Andrew Jackson a national hero.

THE TRAIL OF TEARS

Cherokees had a farm-based economy similar to that of white settlers. They also had a constitutional government much like that of the United States. But European Americans were determined to take Cherokee land for themselves. In 1830, Andrew Jackson, by then the president of the United States, signed the Indian Removal Act. This act stated that all Native Americans east of the Mississippi River would be forced to move west of the Mississippi to Indian Territory, which is now Oklahoma.

Many Cherokees refused to believe that the federal government would force them to leave their homeland.

They asked the government to restore their rights but were bitterly disappointed. After years of threats, in May 1838, 7,000 U.S. soldiers under the command of General Winfield Scott began rounding up Native Americans in Tennessee. Young and old, poor and rich packed whatever possessions they could quickly gather before the soldiers took them to crowded detention camps.

From May 1838 to March 1839, Native Americans walked

Cherokee Indians on the Trail of Tears

MINI-BIO

SEQUOYAH: CHEROKEE LEADER

Sequoyah (c. 1770–1843) was born in a Cherokee town called Tuskegee in East Tennessee. As a young man, he learned how to read and write from Charles Hicks, a wealthy farmer. Sequoyah decided to create a written language for his people. Called Talking Leaves, this language took 12 years to develop. The "leaves" represented syllables in the language. Under Sequoyah's direction, Cherokees printed the first Native American newspaper, called the Cherokee Phoenix. Sequoyah moved west to Arkansas and Oklahoma before the Cherokee were forced to leave their home on the Trail of Tears.

? Want to know more? See http://tennessee encyclopedia.net/imagegallery.php?EntryID=S019

Enslaved Africans worked in cotton fields in Tennessee and many other Southern states.

A notice of land and slaves for sale near Jackson

west through heat, rain, and snow. Many grew sick, and an estimated 4,000 people died before they reached their destination, Indian Territory. This march, which in English is known as the Trail of Tears, is called *Nunna-da-ul-tsun-yi* in the Cherokee language, meaning "the place where they cried."

SLAVERY AND ABOLITION

As Native Americans were forced off their land, white settlers poured into the region. Some white settlers brought enslaved Africans to Tennessee. Because East Tennessee was hilly and only suitable for small farms, many farmers had only one or two enslaved workers.

In Middle Tennessee, landowners planted tobacco and grain and raised livestock. Farms were larger, and many more laborers were needed. Farmers in West Tennessee began growing cotton, using large numbers of enslaved people. In 1800, there were fewer than 4,000 enslaved people in Tennessee. By 1830, that number had risen to 146,158.

Some people in Tennessee thought slavery was wrong. Tennesseans such as Elihu Embree and Benjamin Lundy worked to free enslaved people. Religious groups, particularly Quakers and Presbyterians, started several early antislavery societies that sought to persuade masters to free slaves. By 1826, they had convinced the Tennessee legislature to end the slave trade in the state. The state's wealthy landowners and politicians ignored this law, however.

By 1860, 47 people in Tennessee had more than 100 slaves, and one had more than 300. More than three-fourths of all slaveholders held fewer than 10 slaves. Despite the fact that Tennessee did not depend on slavery as heavily as other Southern states, slave owners controlled the state government.

Andrew Johnson, a poor white tailor from East Tennessee who became president after the Civil War, said that there were 27 poor whites to every slaveholder in Tennessee, "and yet the slave power controlled the state."

PUBLISHER AND ABOLITIONIST

In 1790, Elihu Embree (1782–1820), the son of a Quaker minister, moved with his family from Pennsylvania to northeastern Tennessee. Embree, an iron manufacturer, initially was a slave owner, but he became a committed **abolitionist**. Around 1812, he freed all of the enslaved people who worked for him. In April 1820, he began publishing the *Emancipator* in in Jonesborough. The monthly newspaper went on to become the first U.S. publication devoted exclusively to the antislavery cause.

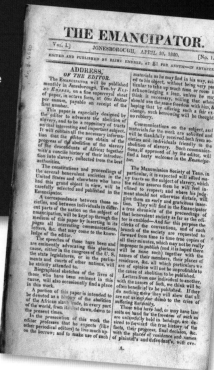

The first page of the first issue of the *Emancipator*, April 1820

WORDS TO KNOW

abolitionist *a person who works to end slavery*

emancipator *a person who frees someone from slavery or some other form of control*

Isham G. Harris, governor of
Tennessee from I857 to I862

WORD TO KNOW

seceding *withdrawing from a*
group or an organization

THE CIVIL WAR

By the mid-1800s, most Northern states had already abolished slavery, but people who held power in the South believed that their economy would crumble without slavery. In 1860, Abraham Lincoln was elected president. Many Southerners believed that he would put an end to slavery, so shortly after the election, Southern states began **seceding** from the Union. They formed their own country, the Confederate States of America. Lincoln did not think states had the right to leave the Union, and he was willing to fight to keep the Union whole. In April 1861, the Civil War began.

As the nation was torn in two, so was Tennessee. West Tennesseans, led by Governor Isham G. Harris, depended heavily on the profits of slavery and supported the Confederacy. Most people in East Tennessee supported the Union. People in Middle Tennessee were divided.

In May 1861, Governor Harris and the legislature declared that Tennessee was independent from the United States and agreed to a military partnership with the Confederacy. The Tennessee government raised an army with the purpose of defending the state against a Union attack. Some counties tried to secede from the state rather than fight for the Confederacy. In Tennessee, the Civil War would truly divide friend from friend, neighbor from neighbor, and father from son.

The Third Battle of Chattanooga, which was fought November 23–25, 1863

Many young Tennesseans volunteered for Confederate army units forming in their hometowns. Those who supported the Union left to join army units in northern states. About 31,000 Tennesseans joined the Union army. Twenty thousand African Americans from Tennessee escaped to freedom and joined the Union army to help free others from slavery and keep the nation whole.

Battles in Tennessee were fierce and bloody. One of the worst took place at Shiloh on April 6, 1862. Confederate troops attacked Union soldiers under the command of Ulysses S. Grant and forced them to retreat to the Tennessee River. Reinforcements soon arrived to help Grant's troops, and as the sun rose on a new day, Grant attacked. Union forces won the battle and forced the Confederate troops into Mississippi. In all, more than 13,000 Union soldiers and nearly 11,000 Confederate troops were killed, wounded, or captured at Shiloh.

By June 1863, Union forces soon occupied most of central Tennessee. In August, Union general Ambrose Burnside and his troops arrived from Kentucky to capture Knoxville. In the eastern third of the state, Union sympathizers felt relief. To their west, Confederate supporters were in despair. The war had lasted more than two years, and no end was in sight.

The war finally ended in 1865. The South had lost. Only Virginia had suffered more battles on its soil than Tennessee. About 66,000 Confederates and 58,000 Union soldiers were killed or wounded in battles in Tennessee. Many more had died of disease or other causes. The Tennessee countryside was in ruins. Railroad lines had been destroyed, and bridges had been bombed. Families had lost husbands, fathers, and sons. There were few healthy mules or horses for farmwork, and there was very little food.

RECONSTRUCTION AND VIOLENCE

After the Civil War, the United States entered a period called Reconstruction, a time of rebuilding. Southern states would be readmitted to the Union after they declared an end to their secession and **ratified** the Thirteenth Amendment, which abolished slavery.

WORD TO KNOW

ratified *formally approved something, such as a legal document*

CIVIL RIGHTS ACTIVIST

Callie House (1861–1928) was a **civil rights** pioneer who promoted African American rights during the era of Jim Crow laws. She worked with Isaiah Dickerson to organize the National Ex-Slave Mutual Relief, Bounty, and Pension Association in 1894. The group gave financial support to formerly enslaved African Americans. House's group cared for those who were sick and disabled and paid for burial expenses. Throughout her life, House worked for the betterment of African Americans.

Much of Tennessee was in ruins at the end of the Civil War.

WORD TO KNOW

civil rights *basic rights that are guaranteed to all people under the U.S. Constitution*

Tennessee took quick action to meet these requirements. On July 24, 1866, Tennessee became the first former Confederate state readmitted to the Union. Because Tennessee also ratified the Fourteenth Amendment, which guaranteed citizenship rights to former slaves, it was the only former Confederate state to which the federal government did not appoint a military governor.

Tennessee faced many challenges. Many men were still recovering from battle wounds or had become disabled during the war. Formerly enslaved people needed help finding jobs and getting an education. It had been illegal to teach enslaved people to read or write, so during Reconstruction the government set up schools to teach reading, writing, and math.

Officials in the Freedmen's Bureau in Memphis explain laws to newly freed African Americans in 1866.

Reconstruction, though, was marked by much violence toward African Americans. Many former slaveholders were angry that the South had lost the war, and they were angry that they had to share power with former slaves. They believed in white supremacy, which is the idea that white people are superior to black people. Many poor whites who had never owned slaves also held these beliefs.

In 1865, former Confederate soldiers founded the Ku Klux Klan (KKK) in Pulaski, Tennessee. Within a year, the KKK became a terrorist force against African Americans and white Americans who helped them. The KKK beat and murdered African Americans who tried to exercise their rights. They wanted to keep African Americans under white control and return the South to the time of slavery.

In the late 19th century, lynching became common. A white mob would seize someone—usually an African American—often claiming the person had committed a crime. Lynching victims were beaten, dragged behind horses or cars, or hanged. Lynch mobs in the South, including Tennessee, killed 2,805 people, roughly one victim every week, between 1882 and 1930. At least 214 people were lynched in Tennessee during this period. No one was ever convicted of participating in a lynching.

SEGREGATION TAKES HOLD

At the end of the 19th century, some white people in Tennessee began changing laws to regain the political and economic power they had lost during Reconstruction. State lawmakers passed laws to control African Americans. These laws, called Jim Crow laws, forced African Americans to live apart from whites. African Americans had to eat in separate restaurants and ride in separate train cars. They could not enter "whites only" restrooms, drink from "whites only" fountains, or seek care in "whites only" hospitals. These and other restrictions created legal

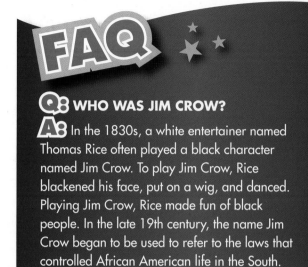

Q: WHO WAS JIM CROW?

A: In the 1830s, a white entertainer named Thomas Rice often played a black character named Jim Crow. To play Jim Crow, Rice blackened his face, put on a wig, and danced. Playing Jim Crow, Rice made fun of black people. In the late 19th century, the name Jim Crow began to be used to refer to the laws that controlled African American life in the South.

JIM CROW LAW.

UPHELD BY THE UNITED STATES SUPREME COURT.

Statute Within the Competency of the Louisiana Legislature and Railroads—Must Furnish Separate Cars for Whites and Blacks.

Washington, May 18.—The Supreme Court today in an opinion read by Justice Brown, sustained the constitutionality of the law in Louisiana requiring the railroads of that State to provide separate cars for white and colored passengers. There was no interstate commerce feature in the case for the railroad upon which the incident occurred giving rise to case—Plessey vs. Ferguson—East Louisiana railroad, was and is operated wholly within the State, to the laws of Congress of many of the States. The opinion states that by the analogy of the laws of Congress, and of many of states requiring establishment of separate schools for children of two races and other similar laws, the statute in question was within competency of Louisiana Legislature, exercising the police power of the State. The judgment of the Supreme Court of State upholding law was therefore upheld.

Mr. Justice Harlan announced a very vigorous dissent saying that he saw nothing but mischief in all such laws. In his view of the case, no power in the land had right to regulate the enjoyment of civil rights upon the basis of race. It would be just as reasonable and proper, he said, for states to pass laws requiring separate cars to be furnished for Catholic and Protestants, or for descendants of those of Teutonic race and those of Latin race.

A newspaper article announcing the result of the *Plessy v. Ferguson* Supreme Court case in 1896

MINI-BIO

IDA B. WELLS-BARNETT: FIGHTING FOR EQUALITY

Ida B. Wells-Barnett (1862–1931), a journalist and civil rights activist, launched an antilynching campaign in the 1890s. She moved from Mississippi to Memphis in 1880 and began attending Fisk University. She soon began publicly fighting segregation laws. When she refused to give up her seat in a train car reserved for whites, three men dragged her out. In 1889, she became the co-owner and editor of Free Speech, a newspaper that challenged segregation. As a newspaper editor, Wells-Barnett also challenged lynchings. She was one of the founders of the National Association of Colored Women and for years toured the world demanding justice and equality for African Americans.

 Want to know more? See www.duke.edu/~ldbaker/ classes/AAIH/caaih/ibwells/ibwbkgrd.html

WORD TO KNOW

segregation *separation from others, according to race, class, ethnic group, religion, or other factors*

segregation. They prevented African Americans from voting and buying homes in white neighborhoods. The laws took away rights that African Americans had gained from President Lincoln before the Civil War ended. Free African Americans were no longer truly free.

In 1896, the U.S. Supreme Court ruled in a case called *Plessy v. Ferguson* that maintaining "separate but equal" facilities for African Americans was legal. In reality, however, the facilities were never equal. Schools for African American children were run-down and poorly funded.

ECONOMIC CHANGES

Tennessee saw major changes in its economy in the years after the Civil War.

Newly freed African Americans owned no land, and many people could not find jobs. By the 1880s, a labor system called sharecropping developed. Sharecroppers rented land from a landowner, who supplied seeds and tools in return for part of the harvest. The sharecropper took all the risks; the landowner usually took all the profits. At the end of each year, sharecroppers frequently found that they actually owed money to the landowners. Because of this, they could not leave the land. They were stuck working for the same landowner year after year,

Tennessee factories, such as this hosiery mill in Loudon, often employed children.

without making any money. Both African American and white sharecroppers were trapped in this system.

During this same period, Tennessee cities began attracting northern companies. The companies moved to the state to take advantage of its cheap labor and low taxes. By 1870, Chattanooga had ironworks, furniture makers, and sawmills. Knoxville and Nashville factories produced flour, paper, soap, and metal goods. Industrial production reached levels far beyond Tennessee's economic output before the war. As the 20th century approached, life was changing in Tennessee.

58

READ ABOUT

Gathering wood
outside a home
in the mountains,
around 1900

1915

*Boll weevils
destroy
Tennessee's
cotton crop*

1916

*Millions of African
Americans begin
moving north in the
Great Migration*

1925 ▶

*John Scopes is tried for
teaching evolution in his
school*

C H A P T E R   F I V E

MORE MODERN TIMES

★

THE EARLY 20TH CENTURY WAS A CHALLENGING PERIOD FOR TENNESSEE. African Americans were trapped in debt, enduring poor education, violence, and unfair laws. Then a beetle called the boll weevil arrived, making life in the South even worse. The boll weevil laid its eggs inside cottonseed pods. When the eggs hatched, the weevils ate the cotton from the inside out. By 1915, boll weevils had eaten their way through most of Tennessee's cotton crops.

1960
Students in Nashville desegregate lunch counters

1991 ▶
Willie W. Herenton is elected the first African American mayor of Memphis

2008
Janice Holder becomes the first female chief justice of the state supreme court

Women canning tomatoes for World War I soldiers

WORLD WAR I

In 1914, World War I began in Europe, and in 1917, the United States joined the war. Eventually, about 60,000 Tennesseans served in the U.S. military during the war.

One of the most decorated soldiers during World War I was Tennessean Alvin C. York. In October 1918, York almost single-handedly defeated a German machine gun battalion. He and his men captured 132 Germans. His actions saved many American lives.

Those who stayed in Tennessee also did their part in the war effort. Citizens bought war bonds, and many people got jobs in factories that produced cloth, weapons, and other goods for the war. Farms grew more crops to supply the military, while families grew Victory Gardens at home so that more farm crops would be available to feed soldiers.

DEMANDING THE RIGHT TO VOTE

In 1919, Congress passed the Nineteenth Amendment, giving women the right to vote. But before it became law, two-thirds of the states had to ratify it. By March 1920, 35 states had ratified it, one less than the two-thirds needed. Tennessee had not yet voted. In Tennessee, the deciding vote was cast by a representative whose mother told him he'd better vote for it! Tennessee ratified the Nineteenth Amendment on August 18, 1920, and women's right to vote became part of the U.S. Constitution.

THE GREAT MIGRATION

In 1900, three-fourths of African Americans in Tennessee were farmworkers, but less than 10 percent owned land. Most of the state's African Americans were trapped in poverty.

World War I increased orders for manufactured goods and processed food, so factories needed more employees. When the war began, immigration from Europe basically stopped, and many workers, mostly white males, joined the military. To fill their urgent need for labor, northern factories opened their doors to African Americans. The factories paid good wages, and African Americans began leaving behind the poverty of the rural South for work in northern cities.

African Americans moved north seeking more than good jobs. They also wanted a better education for their children, access to quality medical care, and freedom from segregation. Between 1916 and 1970, nearly 7 million African Americans headed north in a movement called the Great Migration.

THE GREAT DEPRESSION

After the Great Migration, Tennessee landowners had trouble finding workers for their farms. And in western Tennessee, boll weevils continued destroying cotton crops. The state's economy was already suffering when prices on the New York Stock Exchange crashed

MINI-BIO

ANNE DALLAS DUDLEY: EDUCATOR AND REFORMER

Born to a prominent Nashville family, Anne Dallas Dudley (1876–1955) was a leader in the woman suffrage movement. She was elected president of the Tennessee Equal Suffrage Association in 1915. Five years later, the United States ratified the Nineteenth Amendment, giving women across the nation the right to vote. Dudley then went on to organize the Woman's Civic League of Nashville and worked to educate Tennesseans on public health issues.

❓ **Want to know more?** See http://tennesseeencyclopedia.net/imagegallery.php?EntryID=D059

WORD TO KNOW

suffrage *the right to vote*

62

THE SCOPES TRIAL

In 1925, a trial in Dayton, Tennessee, made headlines around the world. A high school teacher named John Scopes was charged with teaching his biology class that humans had evolved from other animals. At the time, Tennessee's Butler Act forbade public schools from teaching about evolution. Instead, teachers could only discuss the biblical story that God created humans. Two of the nation's top lawyers took part in the trial. William Jennings Bryan, a commanding speaker who had been the Democratic candidate for president three times, served as the prosecutor. Renowned Chicago lawyer Clarence Darrow defended Scopes. During the trial, Bryan and Darrow argued over science and the Bible. People across the nation followed the trial closely. It was even broadcast live over the radio. In the end, Scopes was found guilty and fined $100, but the Tennessee Supreme Court reversed the verdict. The Butler Act stayed on the books until 1967.

Workers for the Works Progress Administration building a road to connect Muscle Shoals Highway with Memphis Highway, 1936

in October 1929, plunging the country further into the Great Depression. All across Tennessee, banks, factories, and farms failed. People were thrown out of work. They could not pay the rent on their homes or buy food for their families. Many people were left homeless and were forced to stand in soup lines to get food.

In 1933, Franklin Roosevelt became president. He soon began a series of programs called the New Deal to help bring some relief to suffering Americans. The Tennessee Valley Authority hired workers to build dams and develop **hydroelectric plants** to provide cheap electricity. The

Works Progress Administration (WPA), a New Deal program, put Tennesseans to work building libraries, roads, and schools. WPA workers erected airports in Memphis, Chattanooga, Knoxville, Nashville, and the Tri-Cities of Bristol, Johnson City, and Kingsport. In 1937, when a flood swept over parts of Memphis, thousands of WPA workers built makeshift **levees** and flood walls to limit water damage. WPA employees also helped care for 50,000 people left homeless by the flood. Another program was the Civilian Conservation Corps (CCC). During the Depression, CCC projects included Great Smoky Mountains National Park and 17 Tennessee state parks.

WORLD WAR II

Although the New Deal programs put some people to work, the Great Depression didn't end until 1939. That year, Great Britain, France, and other nations went to war against Germany, which had invaded neighboring countries. U.S. allies in Europe needed supplies and food, and American factories and farms produced them. Tennessee made cotton for uniforms, food for soldiers, and metal to build weapons and ammunition. The United States joined the war in 1941, and more than 300,000 Tennesseans, both men and women, served in the armed forces.

During the war, many Tennesseans left rural areas to work in factories in the cities. Many women entered the workforce for the first time, taking the place of men who went off to fight. Women worked in plants that manufactured war supplies. By the end of the war, they accounted for one-third of the state's workforce.

Working on an airplane in a Nashville factory, 1943

Some Tennesseans helped to build the first atomic bomb, a single bomb with enough power to destroy an entire city. In Oak Ridge, Tennessee, the U.S. military built a huge complex, including a machine that processed uranium, a metal needed to make the bomb. Uranium from Oak Ridge was used in one of the atomic bombs dropped on Japan to end the war in 1945.

THE CIVIL RIGHTS MOVEMENT

When African American soldiers returned to Tennessee after World War II, they faced the same **discrimination** as when they had left. African American men had fought and died for their country. Women had served as nurses, drivers, and factory workers. Yet African Americans still faced segregation's limits on themselves and their children.

In February 1946, James Stephenson, a 19-year-old navy veteran, was nearly lynched when a white man in a Columbia department store accused Stephenson of attacking him. Stephenson was arrested, and after he was released he fled town. That night African Americans shot and wounded four police officers who tried to enter their business district. The Tennessee Highway Patrol arrived the following morning, firing on buildings, wrecking businesses, and beating and arresting African Americans. Two days later, police killed two of the men they had jailed. The government later found the white police officers not guilty of any crimes. Racial tension in Columbia and elsewhere remained high for months. Soon many Tennesseans, black and white, would begin more active, peaceful protests in the fight for civil rights.

In 1954, the U.S. Supreme Court ruled that "separate but equal" education was not equal at all. The

WORD TO KNOW

discrimination *unequal treatment based on race, gender, religion, or other factors*

THE HIGHLANDER FOLK SCHOOL

The Highlander Folk School, which opened in 1932 near Monteagle, educated ordinary people to be leaders in the civil rights movement. At Highlander, African Americans and whites worked together to devise strategies to fight segregation. Civil rights leaders such as Martin Luther King Jr., Rosa Parks, and Stokely Carmichael all studied at Highlander. Graduate Septima Clark became Highlander's director of education and promoted citizenship schools, which taught African Americans to read so that they would be able to vote.

president ordered school districts across the nation to end segregation, which violated the U.S. Constitution. Many Tennessee schools refused to comply with the order. The following year, several African American families filed a lawsuit in an effort to **desegregate** Nashville public schools. The resulting court case, *Kelly v. Board of Education*, became the longest-running legal case in Tennessee history. As recently as 1996, courts were still determining where African American and white children would attend school.

Other African Americans attempted to peacefully desegregate lunch counters in Nashville. In 1960, black students—including Diane Nash, John Lewis, James Bevel, Cordell Reagon, Matthew Jones, and Bernard Lafayette—went to "whites only" restaurants, sat, and

WORD TO KNOW

desegregate *to end the practice of keeping races separate from each other in education or other community activities*

An employee blocks African Americans from entering a "whites only" lunch counter in Memphis, 1961.

MINI-BIO

DOROTHY L. BROWN: SURGEON AND POLITICIAN

Dorothy Brown (1919—2004) began life with few advantages. She grew up in an orphanage in Troy, New York. Brown craved education, and as a teenager she snuck away to attend the local high school. She graduated at the top of her class, went to college, and then completed medical school in Nashville. But Brown didn't just want to be a doctor—she wanted to be a surgeon. She completed five more years of training to become the first black female surgeon in the South. Brown's determination and dedication helped her break other barriers as well. In 1956, she became the first single woman in Tennessee to adopt a child. And in 1966, she became the first African American woman to win a seat in the Tennessee House of Representatives.

? **Want to know more?** See www.nlm.nih.gov/changingthefaceofmedicine/physicians/biography_46.html

In 1957, Bobby Cain of Clinton, Tennessee, became the first African American student in the South to graduate from a formerly all-white high school.

waited to be served. When the restaurant staff refused to serve the students, the police often removed the protesters by force. After several months, restaurants in Nashville began agreeing to serve black customers. This made Nashville the first major city in the South to desegregate its public facilities.

Change was slowly coming to Tennessee. In 1966, Dorothy Brown became the first African American elected to the Tennessee state legislature since the 1870s. She was also the first black woman ever elected to the state legislature.

On April 4, 1968, civil rights leader Martin Luther King Jr. was in Memphis to support African American sanitation workers, who were striking for treatment equal to their white co-workers. King devoted himself to uniting people and promoting peaceful solutions to the nation's racial problems. Standing on the balcony of the Lorraine Motel, King was assassinated by an escaped convict named James Earl Ray. People all over the world were shocked and saddened. Local leaders worked to calm the unrest as anger raged across the city and the nation.

By the 1990s, a dozen African Americans sat in the state legislature. Memphis elected its first black mayor, Willie W. Herenton, in 1991. In Nashville, African

Residents and tourists enjoy the shops and music clubs on Beale Street in Memphis.

American Emmett Turner was chosen to lead the city's police force. Tennesseans of diverse backgrounds kept hope alive for equality for all.

PROGRESS

As the 20th century ended and the 21st century began, Tennessee was proving itself to be a modern, vibrant place. Businesses were drawn to the state, and Tennesseans were making a name for themselves. Al Gore of Carthage served as vice president from 1993 to 2001, and he was the Democratic candidate for president in 2000. Janice Holder began serving on the Tennessee Supreme Court in 1996 and was named the court's first female chief justice in 2008. Tourists flocked to the state to hear all kinds of music and enjoy the great outdoors.

READ ABOUT

Enjoying the
Jefferson
Street Jazz and
Blues Festival
in Nashville

CHAPTER SIX

PEEPLE

★

TAP YOUR TOES TO THE RAPID RHYTHM OF A BLUEGRASS TUNE. Close your eyes and let the music wash over you as dozens of voices join together in a church choir. Sing along at the Grand Ole Opry, or sway to the rhythms of Beale Street blues or jazz. Tennessee is alive with music, and every tune reflects the unique interests and backgrounds of Tennessee's people.

Young people in front of a roller coaster at Dollywood.

TENNESSEANS FROM ALL OVER

More than three-quarters of Tennesseans are of European descent. Many of the first white people who came to Tennessee traced their roots to England and Scotland. In the mid-1800s, German, French, and Irish settlers followed. African Americans are the next-largest group in Tennessee. Although Hispanics make up only a small part of the population, Latinos are part of the fastest-growing ethnic group in the state. Between 1990 and 2000, Tennessee's Hispanic population rose by 278 percent.

People QuickFacts

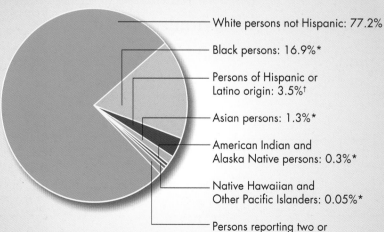

White persons not Hispanic: 77.2%

Black persons: 16.9%*

Persons of Hispanic or Latino origin: 3.5%†

Asian persons: 1.3%*

American Indian and Alaska Native persons: 0.3%*

Native Hawaiian and Other Pacific Islanders: 0.05%*

Persons reporting two or more races: 1.1%

*Includes persons reporting only one race.
†Hispanics may be of any race, so they are also included in applicable race categories.

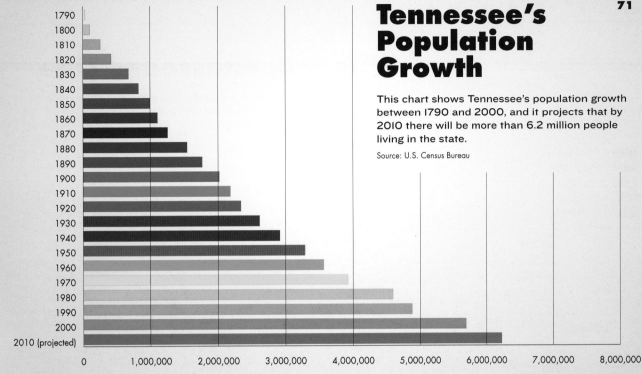

71

Tennessee's Population Growth

This chart shows Tennessee's population growth between 1790 and 2000, and it projects that by 2010 there will be more than 6.2 million people living in the state.

Source: U.S. Census Bureau

Most Latinos in Tennessee come from Mexico, Cuba, or Puerto Rico. A small number of Asian Americans also live in Tennessee.

Tennessee's Native American population numbers about 15,000. Most belong to the Cherokee, Choctaw, or Chickasaw nations. Many Native Americans belong to the Native American Indian Association of Tennessee. This organization helps with job training, education, college scholarships, and health services. It is also a critical part of preserving Tennessee's cultural heritage.

GROWING CITIES

Tennessee's cities are growing much faster than its rural areas. The state's largest cities—Memphis, Nashville, and Knoxville—show the greatest population growth. The suburbs around Nashville and Memphis, the two largest cities, are booming.

Where Tennesseans Live

The colors on this map indicate population density throughout the state. The darker the color, the more people live there.

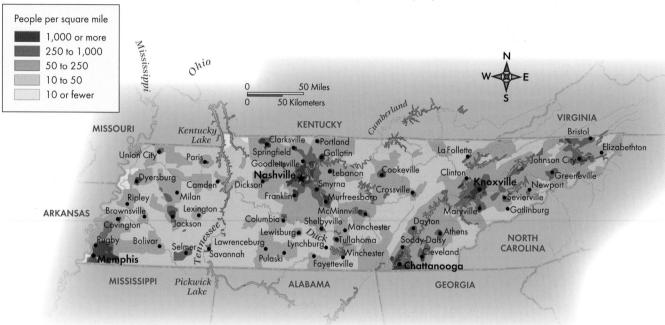

Tennessee's mild winters and pleasant summers combine with relatively low-cost housing to attract senior citizens. The state is becoming a center for retirement. Most senior citizens who move to the state settle in the suburbs near Chattanooga, Nashville, Knoxville, and Memphis.

EDUCATION

In Tennessee, all children between the ages of 6 and 17 must attend school. Most attend public school. The state runs several summer programs for gifted and talented students. These "Governor's Schools" cover subject areas such as agriculture, engineering, technology and computers, arts, and international studies.

Big City Life

This list shows the population of Tennessee's biggest cities.

Memphis	672,227
Nashville	607,413
Knoxville	180,130
Chattanooga	154,762
Clarksville	112,878

Source: U.S. Census Bureau, 2005 estimates

About 10 percent of the children in Tennessee attend private school. Another 3.5 percent are home schooled. State rules require parents or home-school teachers to report attendance, give tests, and teach the subjects required in public and private schools.

Tennessee has many public and private colleges and universities. The largest state-run university is the University of Tennessee system. Its 45,000 undergraduate students and 9,000 graduate students study at campuses in Knoxville, Chattanooga, Martin, Tullahoma, and Memphis. At the University of Tennessee Space Institute, students study and do research in engineering, physics, math, and aviation science.

Among the state's private colleges and universities are Vanderbilt and Fisk universities. Vanderbilt, which is located in Nashville, has outstanding medical and law schools. The college is also home to the Blair School of Music, which attracts gifted students from around the world. Fisk, also in Nashville, opened its doors in 1866. Its first students were newly freed African Americans who ranged in age from 7 to 70.

Tusculum College in Greeneville is the oldest college in Tennessee. It was founded in 1794, two years before Tennessee became a state.

The Bell Tower on the Vanderbilt University campus

WOW

Chattanooga is the home of the MoonPie—a chocolate, graham cracker, and marshmallow snack cake. The MoonPie was first baked in 1917 and is a favorite among Tennesseans of all ages.

Diners at a restaurant in Memphis

HOW TO TALK LIKE A TENNESSEAN

When you're buying a soft drink, order a "coke," not a "soda" or a "pop," even if it's root beer you want. If you're listening to bluegrass music, don't call the four-stringed instrument being played a "violin." Instead, call it a "fiddle." And a "hambone" is not a piece of pork, but a way bluegrass musicians use their hands to slap their chests and thighs to create a rhythm.

HOW TO EAT LIKE A TENNESSEAN

In Tennessee, comfort food is king. Tennessee cooks have the best recipes for corn bread, catfish, fried chicken, and rich, gooey desserts. Down-home cooking is also a specialty at many restaurants. For variety, people also enjoy eating at Japanese, Indian, or Mexican restaurants.

MENU

WHAT'S ON THE MENU IN TENNESSEE?

Pecan pie

Pecan Pie

This pie is the staple dessert of every Tennessee potluck supper. Fill a crust with a mixture of corn syrup, eggs, vanilla, sugar, and pecans and bake until the top is crispy.

Cobbler

This deep-dish dessert features blackberries, cherries, apples, peaches, or plums. Mix the fruit with sugar and a bit of cornstarch, cover with a light biscuit dough, and bake. Serve warm—delicious!

Catfish

Tennessee is known for its catfish. Eat this fish battered and panfried with a side order of corn bread.

Mustard or Collard Greens

Boiled or steamed greens are a must with black-eyed peas, ham, and corn bread. These dishes make up a traditional New Year's dinner.

Tennessee Stack Cake

Stack cake combines dried apples, spices, and a bit of molasses in a breadlike dough. This dish was popular before the Civil War and is still served today.

TRY THIS RECIPE
Corn Bread

Corn bread is a Tennessee favorite, served with almost every dinner. Have an adult nearby when you make this simple recipe.

Ingredients:
1 cup cornmeal
1 cup flour
1 tablespoon baking powder
1 egg
1 cup milk
¼ cup butter, melted

Instructions:
1. Preheat oven to 425°F.
2. Grease a 9-inch square baking pan.
3. In a large bowl, mix the dry ingredients.
4. Add the egg, milk, and melted butter and stir gently until lightly mixed.
5. Pour mixture into baking pan. Bake 20 minutes.
6. When cool enough to touch, cut into squares and dig in!

Corn bread

Carrie Underwood performs with Vince Gill at the Grand Ole Opry in 2008.

SEE IT HERE!

RYMAN AUDITORIUM

In 1892, a riverboat captain named Thomas Ryman opened a performance hall in Nashville called the Union Gospel Tabernacle. After Ryman died in 1904, it was renamed Ryman Auditorium. The 2,362-seat auditorium became a top site for country music concerts, and in 1943 the Grand Ole Opry began broadcasting from there. Over the years, country music legends such as Hank Williams, Patsy Cline, and George Jones performed at Ryman Auditorium. In 1974, the Grand Ole Opry left Ryman for a larger hall, and the auditorium closed for a time, but it has since reopened.

and the Fruit Jar Drinkers. Later, artists such as Roy Acuff, Johnny Cash, Dolly Parton, Hank Williams, and Loretta Lynn began appearing on the Opry and became superstars.

Farther east, in the Appalachians, folk music and bluegrass are popular. Bluegrass music traces its beginnings to Irish, Scottish, and English settlers who brought their traditional music with them. In true bluegrass music, each instrument takes a turn playing the melody while the others provide harmony and rhythm. Every bluegrass group has a fiddle and may also have a bass viol, guitar, banjo, dulcimer, or other stringed instrument. Harmonicas are welcome, and the rhythm is beaten on anything from a washboard to a drum to a pair of spoons.

Clogging, a type of dance, is frequently done to bluegrass music. When cloggers dance, their feet move at an astonishing speed, their toes and heels stomping out the rhythm of the dance.

Dierks Bentley (left) performs with the Grascals bluegrass band at Ryman Auditorium in 2008.

DEFORD BAILEY: STAR OF THE GRAND OLE OPRY

Deford Bailey (1899–1982), born into a musical family east of Nashville, began playing a harmonica as a child. He was the first black musician in the regular cast of the Grand Ole Opry, and he became its biggest star. During his 15 seasons on the Opry, he appeared more times than any other performer. But few listeners knew that this "harmonica wizard" was African American. In 2007, Bailey's signature tune, "Pan American Blues," was inducted into the Grammy Hall of Fame.

? Want to know more? See http://netowne.com/deford/deford.htm

QUILTING FOR A LIFETIME

Ruth Thomas Hale (1919–) has been making quilts all her adult life. Hale has worked with many people to pass on her needle skills. She is an active supporter of the Tennessee 4-H program, which provides clubs for rural children. She is also a guild member of the Cleveland (Tennessee) Museum Center. Every week, she joins other women producing quilts for sick or injured military veterans at Walter Reed Army Medical Center and for cancer patients at St. Jude's Children's Research Hospital in Memphis.

FOLK ARTS AND CRAFTS

Tennessee has a strong tradition of arts and crafts. Quilting and weaving are part of the Tennessee tradition. Many Tennessee quilters and weavers have their works displayed in museums and craft shops. Quilts and hangings are also popular items raffled off for charity.

Woodworking is another Tennessee tradition. Wood turners produce bowls and plates, and whittlers carve pieces of pine or oak into wooden ducks, bears, and other creatures. Some sculptors use chainsaws to hew life-sized black bears from Tennessee tree trunks.

This craftsman is making a musical instrument called a dulcimer.

Author Richard Wright at his desk, 1957

THE WRITTEN WORD

From the days of early settlers to modern times, Tennessee authors and poets have stretched their literary talents. Early tales come to us from George Washington Harris and David "Davy" Crockett. Harris entertained readers with humorous short stories, while Crockett wrote narratives of his adventures on the frontier.

In the early 1900s, Americans enjoyed the poetry and historic writings of John Crowe Ransom, who wrote about home life and southern traditions, and the short stories of Mary Noailles Murfree, who filled her tales with Tennessee mountain folk. Richard Wright's award-winning *Black Boy* takes readers on a journey into the life of an African American child raised in segregated Tennessee.

CHEROKEE POET

Marilou Awiakta (1936–), a member of the Eastern Band of the Cherokee Nation, was born in Oak Ridge. She is a noted poet and public speaker. Awiakta's poetry reflects her Cherokee culture and links Cherokee history to contemporary issues. Her books include *Selu: Seeking the Corn-Mother's Wisdom* and *Rising Fawn and the Fire Mystery*.

MINI-BIO

NIKKI GIOVANNI: POET

Nikki Giovanni (1943–) was born in Knoxville and grew up to become a teacher and a poet. Inspired by African American activists such as Martin Luther King Jr. and Malcolm X, Giovanni often addresses civil rights issues in her poetry. She also frequently touches on family. Giovanni has written several books of poetry for children, including *Spin a Soft Black Song* and *Vacation Time*.

? **Want to know more?** See www.poets.org/poet. php/prmPID/173

The Tennessee Titans in action against the Cleveland Browns, December 2008

Robert Penn Warren, who was a student at Clarksville High School and Vanderbilt University, was a leading poet and novelist of the 20th century. He is the only person to have won the Pulitzer Prize for both fiction and poetry. Other prominent Tennessee poets are Marilou Awiakta, who touches on Cherokee history in her work, and Nikki Giovanni, who writes for both adults and children.

SPORTS

Nashville is home to the Tennessee Titans football team and the Nashville Predators hockey team. In West Tennessee, fans cheer on the Memphis Grizzlies in the National Basketball Association. The West Tenn Diamond Jaxx are a Class AA baseball

The Univeristy of Tennessee women's basketball team facing UCLA, 2007

MINI-BIO

WILMA RUDOLPH: OLYMPIC CHAMPION

Wilma Rudolph (1940–1994) was born into a large family in Clarksville. At age 5, she came down with polio, which crippled her, making her unable to walk on her own. She struggled to strengthen her legs, and by age 12, she was able to get rid of her leg braces. After that, she was constantly on the move. In the 1960 Olympics, Rudolph won the 100-meter, 200-meter, and sprint relay events, making her the first woman to win three gold medals in track-and-field events in the same Olympics.

? **Want to know more?** See www.gale.cengage. com/free_resources/bhm/bio/rudolph_w.htm

team out of Jackson, and the Memphis Redbirds play AAA ball. The eastern part of the state fields a minor league hockey team, the Knoxville Ice Bears.

Colleges field teams in a wide range of sports. The Volunteers of the University of Tennessee have nationally known football, basketball, and women's basketball programs. The state's track-and-field, soccer, and other sports programs have produced many Olympic medal winners, including soccer player Cindy Parlow, sprinter Wilma Rudolph, and rider Melanie Smith.

Auto racing is the most popular spectator sport in Tennessee. The Bristol Motor Speedway and the Nashville Superspeedway host a number of races throughout the year.

READ ABOUT

Members of the Tennessee state senate cast their votes for a lottery scholarship bill in May 2008.

GOVERNMENT

★

THE GOVERNMENT HAS MANY ROLES. It builds roads and runs schools and libraries. It operates courts where people can settle disputes, and it runs programs that help people start small businesses. The government is also involved in keeping people safe and healthy. It does this by providing police and fire protection and making sure that people have clean water to drink. In these ways and many more, the government provides services that Tennesseans want and need.

The capitol in Nashville

Capitol Facts

Here are some fascinating facts about Tennessee's state capitol:

- The capitol was originally designed in 1845.

- The capitol features a square tower with a cupola on top.

- The height of the capitol with the cupola is 170 feet (52 m).

- The building is made of Tennessee marble and limestone.

- The capitol grounds feature statues of prominent Tennesseans, including President Andrew Jackson, President Andrew Johnson, and Alvin York, a World War I hero.

- President James K. Polk and his wife, Sarah, are buried on the capitol grounds.

THE STATE CONSTITUTION

The first Tennessee constitution was written in 1796. The current constitution was adopted in 1870 and was written to end Reconstruction in Tennessee. Tennessee's constitution sets up the government in three branches—executive, judicial, and legislative— with each branch having specific duties and responsibilities to the state's citizens. The constitution also has a bill of rights that lists the rights and freedoms of Tennessee citizens.

Capital City

This map shows places of interest in Nashville, Tennessee's capital city.

EXECUTIVE BRANCH

The governor is the head of the executive branch. In Tennessee, the governor is the only statewide elected official, but many other people also work in the executive branch. Department heads make up a cabinet and provide the governor with advice on matters ranging from agriculture to transportation to issues concerning children. The governor also has advisory boards and commissions that investigate issues and make recommendations on topics such as health care and education. Each of these departments, boards, and commissions has a staff of workers, making the executive branch fairly large.

William Strickland, the state capitol's original architect, died while the capitol was being built. He was buried in the building.

Tennessee State Government

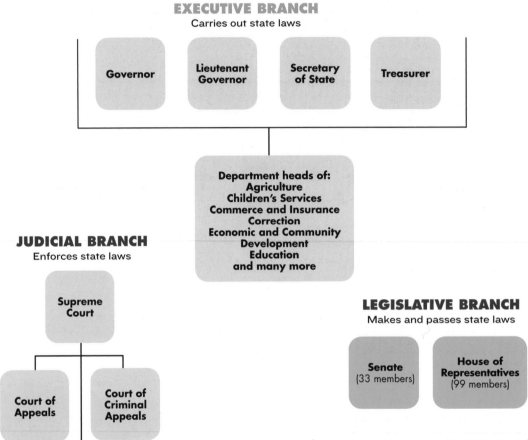

EXECUTIVE BRANCH
Carries out state laws

Governor

Lieutenant Governor

Secretary of State

Treasurer

Department heads of:
Agriculture
Children's Services
Commerce and Insurance
Correction
Economic and Community
Development
Education
and many more

JUDICIAL BRANCH
Enforces state laws

Supreme Court

Court of Appeals

Court of Criminal Appeals

Chancery Courts

Criminal Courts

Circuit Courts

Probate Courts

Municipal Courts

Juvenile Courts

LEGISLATIVE BRANCH
Makes and passes state laws

Senate
(33 members)

House of Representatives
(99 members)

The governor's main responsibility is to carry out the state laws. Enforcing laws costs money, and the governor helps plan how state money is collected and spent. Tennessee's state budget covers costs such as building roads, encouraging tourism, and funding state police. According to law, Tennessee's budget must be balanced every year. The state cannot spend more money than it collects from taxes and other sources.

State legislators watch as Governor Phil Bredesen signs a bill in May 2005.

Tennessee's governor is the commander in chief of the state's National Guard and can call on the guard in the event of an emergency. He or she also represents the interests of Tennessee at meetings with other governors and national officials, as well as with business leaders interested in setting up factories or offices in Tennessee. The governor appoints judges and department leaders, who must be approved by the legislature. Tennessee's governors are elected to four-year terms, and they are limited to two terms in office.

LEGISLATIVE BRANCH

The Tennessee legislature is made up of two parts, the senate and the house of representatives. Together they are called the General Assembly. The senate has 33

Representing Tennessee

This list shows the number of elected officials who represent Tennessee, both on the state and national levels.

OFFICE	NUMBER	LENGTH OF TERM
State senators	33	4 years
State representatives	99	2 years
U.S. senators	2	6 years
U.S. representatives	9	2 years
Presidential electors	11	—

members who serve four-year terms. The house has 99 members who serve two-year terms. All members of the General Assembly must be U.S. citizens, have lived in Tennessee for three years, and have lived in the district they are serving for one year. Senators must be at least 30 years old, and representatives must be at least 21 years old.

The General Assembly is responsible for making the state laws. This is neither an easy nor a quick task. Suppose a senator submits a bill, or proposed law. The bill is sent to the most appropriate committee to be studied and discussed. For example, a bill related to farming would be sent to the agriculture committee. If the committee approves of the bill, it will be discussed by the entire senate. If the senate votes in

Governor Phil Bredesen addresses a joint session of the General Assembly in May 2008.

favor of the bill, it is sent to the house of representatives for a second vote. Bills that pass both houses go to the governor to be signed. A signed bill becomes a law. If the governor rejects, or vetoes, the bill, it fails. A bill can also become a law if the governor fails to take action within 10 business days.

JUDICIAL BRANCH

The judicial branch consists of the state's court system. The state is divided into 31 judicial districts. Each district has a chancery court and a circuit court. The chancery courts hear cases that deal with issues such as the constitution, appointing guardians for children, and real estate sales. Circuit courts hear both civil and criminal cases. A criminal trial might involve a robbery, whereas a civil trial deals with lawsuits such as one person accusing another of not fulfilling a contract. Thirteen of the judicial districts also have criminal courts. A criminal court hears trials concerning crimes such as theft, murder, or assault.

Tennessee has two **appeals** courts. The 12-member court of appeals is responsible for reviewing decisions made in civil cases, and the 12-member court of criminal appeals reviews criminal cases. The supreme court is the highest court in the state. It has five judges, called justices. The supreme court decides whether laws violate the state constitution and reviews decisions made in lower courts.

When a vacancy occurs on the supreme court or one of the appeals courts, a commission made up of members of both political parties makes a list of three nominees to fill the seat. The governor chooses one of the nominees to serve an eight-year term. Every eight years, voters decide whether or not to keep the judge.

Andrew Johnson of Tennessee was the only president to later serve in the U.S. Senate.

WACKY LAWS

Tennessee has some pretty weird laws! These may still be on the books, but do you think they're enforced?

- It is illegal to use a lasso to catch fish.
- It is against the law to drive a car while sleeping.
- In Memphis restaurants, it is illegal to give any pie to fellow diners, and it's illegal to take unfinished pie home.

WORD TO KNOW

appeals *legal proceedings in which a court is asked to change the decision of a lower court*

Tennessee Counties

This map shows the 95 counties in Tennessee. Nashville, the state capital, is indicated with a star.

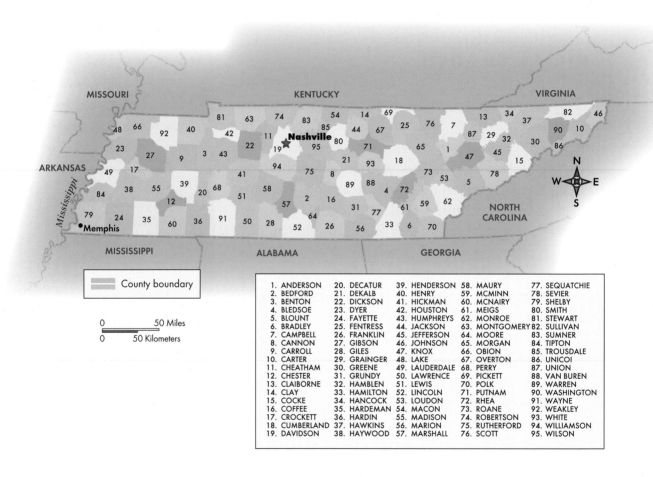

County boundary

0   50 Miles
0   50 Kilometers

1. ANDERSON	20. DECATUR	39. HENDERSON	58. MAURY	77. SEQUATCHIE	
2. BEDFORD	21. DEKALB	40. HENRY	59. MCMINN	78. SEVIER	
3. BENTON	22. DICKSON	41. HICKMAN	60. MCNAIRY	79. SHELBY	
4. BLEDSOE	23. DYER	42. HOUSTON	61. MEIGS	80. SMITH	
5. BLOUNT	24. FAYETTE	43. HUMPHREYS	62. MONROE	81. STEWART	
6. BRADLEY	25. FENTRESS	44. JACKSON	63. MONTGOMERY	82. SULLIVAN	
7. CAMPBELL	26. FRANKLIN	45. JEFFERSON	64. MOORE	83. SUMNER	
8. CANNON	27. GIBSON	46. JOHNSON	65. MORGAN	84. TIPTON	
9. CARROLL	28. GILES	47. KNOX	66. OBION	85. TROUSDALE	
10. CARTER	29. GRAINGER	48. LAKE	67. OVERTON	86. UNICOI	
11. CHEATHAM	30. GREENE	49. LAUDERDALE	68. PERRY	87. UNION	
12. CHESTER	31. GRUNDY	50. LAWRENCE	69. PICKETT	88. VAN BUREN	
13. CLAIBORNE	32. HAMBLEN	51. LEWIS	70. POLK	89. WARREN	
14. CLAY	33. HAMILTON	52. LINCOLN	71. PUTNAM	90. WASHINGTON	
15. COCKE	34. HANCOCK	53. LOUDON	72. RHEA	91. WAYNE	
16. COFFEE	35. HARDEMAN	54. MACON	73. ROANE	92. WEAKLEY	
17. CROCKETT	36. HARDIN	55. MADISON	74. ROBERTSON	93. WHITE	
18. CUMBERLAND	37. HAWKINS	56. MARION	75. RUTHERFORD	94. WILLIAMSON	
19. DAVIDSON	38. HAYWOOD	57. MARSHALL	76. SCOTT	95. WILSON	

LOCAL GOVERNMENT

Tennessee is divided into 95 counties. Most of the counties are governed by justices of the peace or county chairpeople. Some also have county commissions. A mayor and a city council govern most cities and towns in Tennessee.

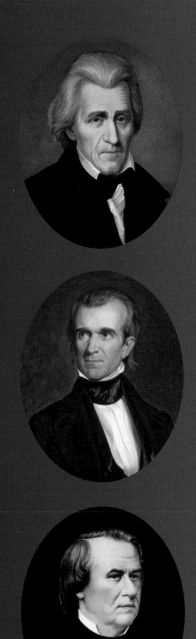

TENNESSEE'S PRESIDENTS

Andrew Jackson (1767–1845) was born in South Carolina and moved to Tennessee later in life. He became a national hero after defeating the British at the Battle of New Orleans during the War of 1812. In 1829, Jackson became the seventh president of the United States. He was the first president to come from a poor background, and he was often considered a tough "man of the people." As president, he opposed a national bank for the United States because he believed it put too much power in the hands of a small group of men. He also signed the Indian Removal Act, forcing all Native Americans in the East to move west.

James K. Polk (1795–1849) was born in North Carolina. He attended the University of North Carolina before moving to Tennessee and becoming a congressman, governor, and, in 1845, the 11th president of the United States. He secured U.S. control over the Pacific Northwest. He also led the country into the Mexican-American War, which resulted in the United States gaining California and much of the Southwest from Mexico.

Andrew Johnson (1808–1875) was born in North Carolina and had no formal education. After moving to Tennessee, he became, in turn, a mayor, a congressman, governor, and U.S. senator. He served as vice president during the Civil War and became the 17th president when Abraham Lincoln was assassinated in 1865. As president, he was wildly unpopular with Congress and was nearly removed from office.

State Flag

LeRoy Reeves, a soldier from Tennessee, designed the state flag, which was adopted on April 17, 1905. In the center of the flag are three white stars in a circle of blue. A field of red surrounds the circle, while a stripe of blue runs down one side. The three stars represent Tennessee's three geographical divisions: West Tennessee, Middle Tennessee, and East Tennessee. The color white symbolizes purity, blue stands for the love Tennesseans have for their home, and red represents their patriotism.

State Seal

When Tennessee wrote its first constitution, its founders provided for an official great seal. The seal's design has changed, but it has kept the figures of a plow, a sheaf of wheat, and a cotton plant, which are all important to the state's agriculture. Above these images is the Roman numeral XVI, which indicates that Tennessee was the 16th state to join the Union. The words *Agriculture* and *Commerce* appear on the seal along with a picture of a boat, which indicates that river trade was long important to the state. Around the outside of the seal are the words *The Great Seal of the State of Tennessee*. The current seal was adopted in 1987.

READ ABOUT

A researcher measures a hemlock tree in Great Smoky Mountains National Park.

C H A P T E R E I G H T

ECONOMY

★

L IKE THEIR FARMER ANCESTORS, THE PEOPLE OF TENNESSEE STILL GROW COTTON AND RAISE CHICKENS. But these days, they also build cars, mine coal, and work in offices. Since the end of World War II, Tennesseans have made more money from industry than agriculture. Farmers, miners, factory workers, businesspeople—they all contribute to the state's economy.

Dr. Henry Moses prepares to teach a dentistry class at Meharry Medical School in Nashville.

SERVING OTHERS

More Tennesseans work in service industries than in any other part of the economy. Service workers, such as doctors, teachers, and bankers, do things for people.

The largest express delivery company in the world is FedEx, which is headquartered in Memphis. The company began in April 1973 with 14 aircraft flying out of Memphis International Airport. FedEx provides a service: It delivers letters and packages overnight for a fee. The service requires trucks, planes, and plenty of people.

Tourists require a wide range of service workers. Hotel clerks check them in, waiters bring their food, and guides show them around. Tourists also buy products in stores. The clerks who wait on them record the sales in computers, and computer technicians keep the computers working smoothly. All of these people work in service industries. Bus drivers, librarians, real estate agents, and receptionists are also service workers.

Music is one of Tennessee's major service industries. CD sales, download sales, and concerts bring money to the state. Every performer has a host of support personnel, including agents, lawyers, recording studio technicians, other musicians, and video producers. The Country Music Television network and the Country Music Hall of Fame both make their home in Nashville. Country music venues such as the Grand Ole Opry attract tourist dollars and provide jobs for many workers.

FROM THE FARM
Farms take up roughly 44 percent of Tennessee's total land area. On the state's 79,000 farms, farmers produce a wide variety of grain and vegetable crops. Cotton, tobacco, and soybeans are the most valuable crops. The state also produces large quantities of greenhouse

MINI-BIO

DOLLY PARTON: SINGER AND BUSINESSPERSON

Sevier County native Dolly Parton (1946–) is a country music star, but she is also a canny businessperson who brought jobs and prosperity to her East Tennessee home. Parton has been producing hit songs since 1966. In 1986, she took over a failing amusement park in Pigeon Forge and turned the place into Dollywood, an amusement park that also features concerts and demonstrations of traditional crafts. This growing attraction provides jobs for locals and boosts the tourist industry in the Great Smoky Mountains.

 Want to know more? See http://lcweb2.loc.gov/diglib/ihas/loc.natlib.ihas.200152702/default.html

Soybeans are Tennessee's most versatile crop. They are used to make cattle feed, oil, medicine, printing ink, paint, cosmetics, and tofu. Research is under way to use soybeans to make an alternative fuel to gasoline.

MINI-BIO

SAM PHILLIPS: FOUNDER OF SUN RECORDS

Born in Florence, Alabama, Sam Phillips (1923–2003) opened the Memphis Recording Service studio in 1950 on a shoestring budget. His goal was to record local talent and release their music for sale. Phillips soon began his own record label, Sun Records, and recorded artists such as Jerry Lee Lewis, Johnny Cash, and Roy Orbison. Sun's recordings of "Don't Be Cruel" and "Hound Dog" by Elvis Presley topped the charts in 1956. In 1969, Phillips sold Sun Records, but his place in music history was secure.

? **Want to know more?** See www.rockhall.com/inductee/sam-phillips

SEE IT HERE!

AGRICULTURAL FAIRS

Each year, Tennessee holds dozens of county, state, and regional agricultural fairs—events dedicated to all things farming. Some fairs display antique tractors and farm equipment along with new models of tractors, pickers, harvesters, and combines. Events range from education about poultry to logging competitions. Visitors can learn about cattle, horses, and hogs, as well as less common farm creatures such as llamas, alpacas, and ostriches!

or nursery products, such as flowers, shrubs, and trees.

Many Tennessee farmers raise livestock. Cattle and calves, chickens, pigs, and hogs are big money-makers. Across the state, livestock producers handle 2.1 million head of cattle, 230,000 pigs, and 2.2 million chickens each year. Tennessee dairy farms produce 1.4 million pounds (635,000 kilograms) of milk each year, which is sold or turned into cheese, yogurt, ice cream, and sour cream. Poultry farms produce 278 million eggs yearly. That's a lot of omelets!

Tennessee ranches raise some 190,000 horses, many belonging to a breed called the Tennessee walking horse. These horses were bred to work fields in the daytime yet give their owners a comfortable ride in the evenings. Tennessee walking horses can be found in the show jumping ring or working on ranches or even in the movies. Many of the horses ridden by television and movie cowboys have been Tennessee walking horses. These horses get their breed name from their unusual "running walk."

A little more than half of Tennessee is covered by forests, and timber production contributes greatly to the state's economy. Yearly, Tennessee forests provide about 225 million board feet (19 million cubic

Tennessee walking horses are known for being calm and easy to train.

feet) of hardwood timber such as oak and 99 million board feet (8 million cu ft) of softwoods such as pine. It ranks as the number one U.S. state in producing hardwood flooring. The timber industry provides jobs for more than 60,000 Tennesseans.

WOW

Silver, the horse ridden by the Lone Ranger on the classic TV show, was a Tennessee walking horse.

Top Products

Agriculture Tobacco, cotton, soybeans, corn, cattle and calves, hogs, chickens

Manufacturing Chemical products, foods, transportation equipment, automobiles, industrial machinery, rubber and plastic goods, paper and paper products

Mining Coal, zinc, crushed stone, freshwater pearls, ball clay, and aluminum

THE TVA

The Tennessee Valley Authority (TVA) was founded by Congress in 1933 as part of President Franklin Roosevelt's New Deal. The purpose of the TVA was to reduce flooding, improve navigation along the Tennessee River, help farmers, and produce inexpensive electric power. Today, the TVA supplies electricity to 8.7 million people. The TVA manages 49 dams, 29 of which produce hydroelectric power. The TVA is the nation's largest public power producer, generating $9 billion in power sales yearly.

MADE IN TENNESSEE

Many kinds of products are made in Tennessee, including cloth, machinery, and processed foods such as bread, breakfast cereal, candy, and cheese.

In the 1980s, several automobile production plants opened in the state. Nissan opened the state's first auto plant in the city of Smyrna in 1983, and four years later, General Motors built a Saturn auto plant in Spring

Workers on an assembly line at the Nissan Motor Company plant in Decherd

Hill. Since then, the Tennessee Valley has become the nation's second-largest auto manufacturing region. In 2006, Nissan relocated the headquarters of its U.S. operations to Franklin, Tennessee. More than 90,000 people now work in Tennessee's automotive industry.

Another successful industry in Tennessee is chemical processing. Tennessee produces industrial chemicals for cleaning, finishing metal goods, and plastic products. The state also produces medicines, paint, soap, and dyes.

MINING

Tennessee ranks first among the states in the production of ball clay and gemstones. Ball clay production is valued at approximately $30 million annually. Ball clay is used in floor tiles, pottery, and bathroom fixtures. The major gemstones produced in Tennessee are mother-of-pearl and freshwater pearls from mussel shells.

Tennessee ranks 19th in the nation in coal production. In Tennessee, coal is mined at surface mines. Rather than removing the coal through tunnels dug into the ground, the rock on the surface of the earth is removed to expose the coal underneath. The state requires that mine owners return the land to its previous condition after the mining is complete. The companies must replant forestland and clean up water pollution.

Crushed stone is one of the leading nonfuel products mined in Tennessee. Tennesseans mine zinc in Knox and Jefferson counties. Other products mined in the state include fuller's earth, sand and gravel, and barite, a mineral used in the manufacture of paints and paper.

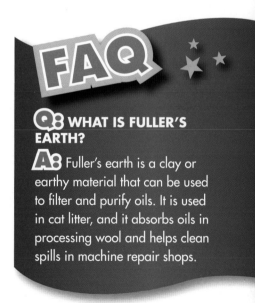

FAQ

Q8 WHAT IS FULLER'S EARTH?

A8 Fuller's earth is a clay or earthy material that can be used to filter and purify oils. It is used in cat litter, and it absorbs oils in processing wool and helps clean spills in machine repair shops.

Major Agricultural and Mining Products

This map shows where Tennessee's major agricultural and mining products come from. See a cow? That means cattle are raised there.

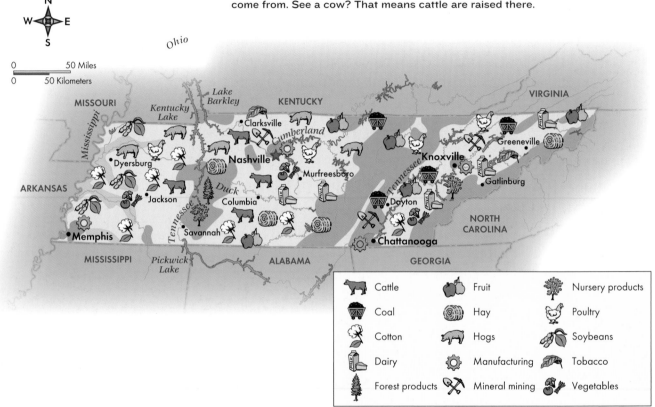

ECONOMIC ADVANTAGES

Tennessee attracts new industries by providing a wide range of benefits for businesses. The state has low utility costs and low taxes. There is no state property tax, and the state gives businesses a tax credit for investments.

The state is centrally located and easily accessible. Shipping on the Mississippi River is an attraction for businesses in the Memphis area. Memphis, Nashville, and Knoxville have major air terminals, and rail lines and freeways crisscross the state.

A skilled employee base adds to the state's economic appeal. State vocational and technical colleges work with local businesses to train potential employees in many fields. People in Tennessee can generally find affordable housing, and the cost of living is low. This makes the state attractive to companies and the employees they hire.

What Do Tennesseans Do?

This color-coded chart shows what industries Tennesseans work in.

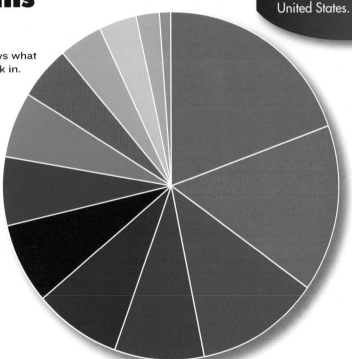

FAQ

Q8 WHERE CAN YOU FIND PEARLS IN LANDLOCKED TENNESSEE?

A8 Pearls are harvested from oysters and other mussels. The American Pearl Company, based in Nashville, operates one of the few freshwater pearl farms in the United States.

19.6% Educational services, health care, and social assistance, 541,411

15.4% Manufacturing, 426,666

12.2% Retail trade, 337,012

8.5% Professional, scientific, management, administrative, and waste management services, 235,974

8.2% Arts, entertainment, recreation, accommodation, and food services, 227,211

7.7% Construction, 211,967

6.4% Transportation, warehousing, and utilities, 176,942

6.1% Finance, insurance, real estate, rental, and leasing, 168,738

5.0% Other services, except public administration, 138,906

4.2% Public administration, 114,714

3.6% Wholesale trade, 100,710

2.0% Information, 55,292

1.1% Agriculture, forestry, fishing, hunting, and mining, 31,352

Source: U.S. Census Bureau, 2006 estimate

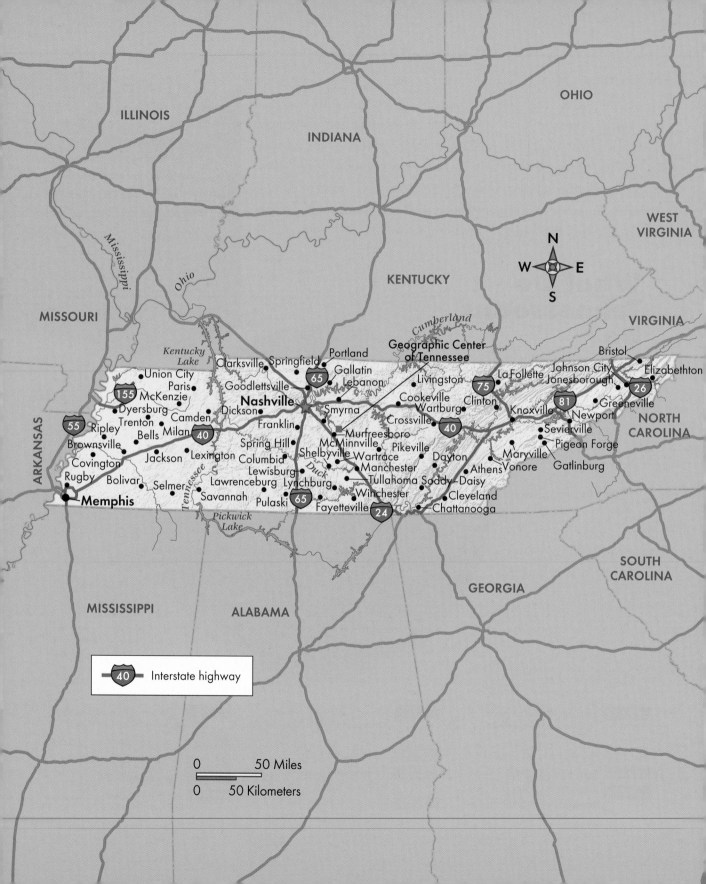

MISSOURI

ILLINOIS

INDIANA

OHIO

WEST VIRGINIA

KENTUCKY

VIRGINIA

Mississippi

Ohio

Kentucky Lake

Clarksville

Springfield

Portland

Geographic Center of Tennessee

Cumberland

Bristol

Union City

Paris

Goodlettsville

65

Gallatin

Lebanon

Livingston

La Follette

75

Johnson City

Jonesborough

Elizabethton

26

McKenzie

Nashville

Cookeville

Wartburg

Clinton

Knoxville

81

Greeneville

155

Dyersburg

Trenton

Camden

Dickson

Smyrna

Crossville

40

Newport

NORTH CAROLINA

Ripley

Milan

Franklin

Murfreesboro

Sevierville

Bells

Spring Hill

McMinnville

Pikeville

Dayton

Pigeon Forge

55

Brownsville

Jackson

Lexington

Columbia

Shelbyville

Wartrace

Maryville

Vonore

Gatlinburg

Covington

Lewisburg

Duck

Manchester

Athens

Rugby

Bolivar

Selmer

Lawrenceburg

Lynchburg

Tullahoma

Soddy-Daisy

Memphis

Savannah

Pulaski

65

Winchester

Cleveland

Tennessee

Fayetteville

24

Chattanooga

Pickwick Lake

MISSISSIPPI

ALABAMA

GEORGIA

SOUTH CAROLINA

40 —— Interstate highway

0   50 Miles

0   50 Kilometers

N W E S

CHAPTER NINE

TRAVEL GUIDE

★

IT'S TIME TO TAKE A TOUR. Pack your bags and let's travel to Tennessee! We'll head into the mountains, travel underground, and float down a river or two. We'll start this tour where the Europeans first entered Tennessee: in the Appalachian Mountains. Ready? Then let's go!

← Follow along with this travel map. We'll start in Gatlinburg and end our trip in Camden.

EAST TENNESSEE

THINGS TO DO: Hike the Great Smokies, splash in the Obed River, or watch speed demons race around the Bristol Speedway.

Gatlinburg

★ **Arrowmont School:** This folk arts center features gallery displays of quilting, weaving, pottery, and woodworking by local artists. It also holds classes.

★ **Great Smoky Mountains National Park:** The Great Smoky Mountains teem with wildlife, rugged trails, and rushing rivers. For folks who enjoy the outdoors, this park is stunning every season of the year. Many say autumn is the best, when colorful leaves paint the mountains rich reds, yellows, and golds.

Great Smoky Mountains National Park

SEE IT HERE!

NATIONAL STORYTELLING FESTIVAL
Each October, 10,000 people gather in Jonesborough for the National Storytelling Festival. Festivalgoers hear tale-twisters, cowboy poets, and many others. The festival offers workshops on how to keep an audience fascinated by fables, folktales, fairy tales, and ghost stories.

Wartburg

★ **Obed Wild and Scenic River:** The Obed River is great for white-water rafting, kayaking, and canoeing. Those who don't want to get wet might want to try rock climbing, hiking, or picnicking. Stop by the scenic overlook at Lilly Bluff for a panoramic view of the Appalachian region.

Vonore

★ **Sequoyah Birthplace Museum:** This museum presents visitors with a wide range of information on Overhill Cherokee history, culture, and archaeology. The site honors Sequoyah, a member of the Cherokee Nation who developed a written Cherokee language.

★ **Fort Loudoun State Park:** Here you can learn about trade in the mid-18th century and the Cherokee ways of life.

Knoxville

★ **Knoxville Zoo:** This zoo houses more than 800 animals from around the world. Popular exhibits include Black Bear Falls, Chimp Ridge, and Grasslands Africa.

★ **East Tennessee Discovery Center:** The Discovery Center presents the wonders of science for children through hands-on displays. The center's Akima Planetarium takes visitors on trips to the stars.

Sevierville

★ **NASCAR SpeedPark:** Here drivers of all ages can experience the excitement of speeding around a racetrack. The park has eight heart-pumping tracks as well as an indoor climbing wall, children's rides, and games.

Bristol

★ **Bristol Motor Speedway:** Known as the "World's Fastest Half-Mile," Bristol Motor Speedway draws 160,000 fans who watch drivers race around the oval.

A roller coaster at Dollywood

Pigeon Forge

★ **Dollywood:** Named after country music star Dolly Parton, Dollywood is billed as the Smoky Mountain Family Adventure. It is Tennessee's biggest attraction. The park has rides, music shows, restaurants, crafts demonstrations, and a host of activities for the entire family.

Clinton

★ **Museum of Appalachia:** Roll up your sleeves and prepare for some down-home fun. This 65-acre (26 ha) working rural farm village is loaded with animals, gardens, and interest. It features 30 old-style cabins and buildings.

Fall Creek Falls State Park

Pikeville

★ **Fall Creek Falls State Park:**
This park has waterfalls, rushing
cascades, sparkling streams, deep
gorges, and well-groomed trails.
Fall Creek Falls drops 256 feet (78
m) into a shaded pool at the base
of its gorge. The park has three
other falls—Piney, Cane Creek, and
Cane Creek Cascades. Bring your
camera—this place is gorgeous.

Chattanooga

★ **Hunter Museum of American
Art:** This museum sits on a bluff
high above the Tennessee River.
It contains an outstanding collection of American art from colonial
times to the present.

★ **Houston Museum of Decorative
Arts:** The Houston is one woman's
collection of 18th-, 19th-, and early
20th-century decorative art objects.
You'll find intricately shaped glass,
classic pottery, and hand-carved
furniture.

★ **Creative Discovery Museum:**
This place is designed especially
for kids 12 and under, although
adults find the interactive displays equally fascinating. In this
museum, kids can dig for dinosaur
bones or sail boats through locks
and dams on a make-believe river.

★ **Dragon Dreams Museum:** You do
not need to be a fairy princess or a
valiant knight to enjoy this unique
exhibition of more than 6,000 drag-
ons from around the world.

★ **Chattanooga African American
Museum:** This museum has
exhibits on everything from blues
legend Bessie Smith to what life
was like for people in East Africa
before they were enslaved.

**On a clear day, you can see
seven states from Chattanooga's
Lookout Mountain.**

Tennessee Aquarium

★ **Tennessee Aquarium:** If you have ever dreamed of swimming near a tropical coral reef, you can experience the next best thing at the Tennessee Aquarium. The coral reef exhibit features parrot fish, seahorses, and much more.

MIDDLE TENNESSEE

THINGS TO DO: Explore caves, ride on a riverboat, or tap your foot to country-and-western tunes.

Nashville

★ **Tennessee State Museum:** This museum displays everything from mastodon bones to Civil War weapons to banners supporting woman suffrage in Tennessee.

★ **Nashville Zoo:** The zoo features hundreds of creatures ranging from insects to elephants. The property also includes the Jungle Gym, a massive playground built by 6,000 volunteers.

★ **Frist Center for the Visual Arts:** This museum showcases the finest in regional art and hosts exhibits of outstanding art from around the world. It also has a large gallery where children can sit down and create some art themselves.

★ *General Jackson* **Showboat:** In the late 1800s, riverboats sailed on several Tennessee rivers. The *General Jackson* is a 300-foot (91 m) paddle wheel riverboat that cruises the Cumberland River all year.

★ **Fisk University Galleries:** These galleries boast works by artists such as Aaron Douglas, Georgia O'Keeffe, and Pablo Picasso.

★ **Musicians Hall of Fame and Museum:** The site honors performers in country, rhythm and blues, soul, funk, jazz, rock, and pop. It focuses on the musicians who have played with top singers and bands.

Lebanon

★ **Fiddlers Grove Historical Village:** This site contains dozens of original and reproduced buildings from more than 100 years ago.

★ **Country Music Hall of Fame and Museum:** Nashville is the country music capital of the world, so it makes sense that the Country Music Hall of Fame and Museum would be one of the city's main attractions. The museum's main building has windows that look like a piano keyboard. Inside, you can learn about and listen to stars such as Johnny Cash, Merle Haggard, and Dolly Parton.

Cheekwood Botanical Garden and Museum of Art

★ **Cheekwood Botanical Garden and Museum of Art:** Cheekwood features a series of gardens and green-houses with thousands of flowers and shrubs. It also includes a gallery that features work by artists such as Jamie Wyeth, Andy Warhol, and Tennessee's own Robert Ryman.

★ **Parthenon:** This building is a full-scale replica of a temple built more than 2,400 years ago in ancient Greece. Today, Nashville's Parthenon is an art museum.

McMinnville

★ **Cumberland Caverns:** This series of caverns makes up Tennessee's largest cave and is a U.S. National Natural Landmark. The cave features under-ground waterfalls and deep pools. Guides give tours that focus on the caverns' many formations.

MINI-BIO

ROBERT RYMAN: NASHVILLE ARTIST

Born in Nashville, Robert Ryman (1930–) is an artist of many talents. He has been a jazz musician, a member of the Army Reserve, and a painter. Ryman experimented with stripping painting down to its most basic elements, sometimes using only one color. His art hangs in the Guggenheim Museum in New York City, the Tate gallery in London, and other museums around the world.

❓ **Want to know more?** See www.guggenheimcollection.org/site/artist_bio_140.html

SEE IT HERE!

ROLLEY HOLE MARBLES CHAMPIONSHIP

Polish up the aggie and practice up for plinko because the National Rolley Hole Marbles Championship is held each September at Standing Stone State Park near Livingston. There's bluegrass music to keep things lively, and demonstrations show how marbles are made. Kids can learn how to shoot a marble or participate in marble games and marble hunts.

Clarksville

★ **Dunbar Cave State Natural Area:** This park is filled with caves and sinkholes. The mouth of Dunbar Cave is so large that people once held square dances, radio shows, and concerts there.

National Civil Rights Museum

WEIRD AND WACKY WONDERS

- Salt and Pepper Shaker Museum, Gatlinburg
- UFO House, Chattanooga
- World's Largest Guitar, Bristol
- World's Largest Teapot Collection, Trenton
- Strolling Jim the Horse, Wartrace

World's Largest Guitar

WEST TENNESSEE

THINGS TO DO: Watch the duck parade at the Peabody, enjoy a day on the river, and tour Graceland, the home of Elvis Presley.

Memphis

★ **National Civil Rights Museum:** This museum brings to life the African American struggle for civil rights from the days of slavery through today.

The White House is the only American home to see more visitors each year than Graceland.

★ **A. Schwab Dry Goods Store:**
This general store first opened its doors in 1876 and has been family owned and operated ever since. The store sells everything from penny candy to 99-cent neckties to voodoo potions.

★ **Peabody Hotel:** This hotel provides elegant, old-fashioned hospitality. Be sure to watch for the parade of ducks that walks through the lobby each day.

FAQ

Q: WHAT ARE THE PEABODY DUCKS?

A: In 1932, the Peabody Hotel's general manager Frank Schutt and a friend played a joke—they put live ducks in the fountain of the hotel's grand lobby. Hotel guests were thrilled. Since then, ducks have been a part of the Peabody experience. Every day at 11 A.M., a flock of ducks follows the Peabody duckmaster down the elevator to the marble fountain in the grand lobby. A red carpet is unrolled, and the ducks march down the carpet to the sound of a brass band playing "King Cotton March." The ducks pass through again at 5 P.M., heading for their home on the roof and a good night's rest.

Graceland

★ **Elvis Presley's Graceland:**
Once the home of Elvis Presley, Graceland has become a museum dedicated to the life of the rock 'n' roll legend. After touring Presley's home, visit the Elvis Auto Museum. Real Elvis fans should be sure to stay across the street at Elvis Presley's Heartbreak Hotel.

★ **Pink Palace Museum:** This museum has exhibits on the culture and natural history of the Tennessee region.

★ **Brooks Museum of Art:** The oldest and largest art museum in Tennessee, the Brooks Museum features collections of Italian, British, and African art.

- ★ **Sharpe Planetarium:** Here you can explore the planets, stars, and our own galaxy, the Milky Way.
- ★ **Beale Street Historic District:** Beale Street has been a center of African American music since the early 20th century. Today, the historic district boasts music clubs, galleries, and restaurants.
- ★ **Mud Island River Park:** Head to the river for a day of recreation and education, all dealing with the Mississippi River. Mud Island has kayak and bike rentals, gift shops and restaurants, and a 5,000-seat amphitheater where you can see plays and concerts.

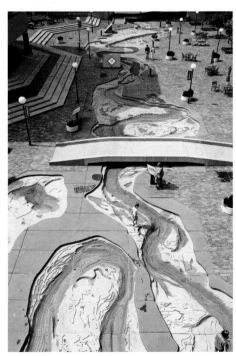

Mud Island River Park

Rugby

- ★ **Historic Rugby:** Step into the late 1800s at this restored British-style village that boasts 20 buildings from the era. Be sure to visit the Hughes Library—named for British author and social reformer Thomas Hughes, who founded the Rugby Colony in 1880.

Bells

- ★ **Cotton Museum of the South:** This museum is located in an old rural village that features a country church, log cabins, and a one-room schoolhouse.

Paris

- ★ **Tennessee National Wildlife Refuge:** Dams on the Tennessee River have created many beautiful lakes. The largest is Kentucky Lake in northwestern Tennessee, where people can fish, boat, and enjoy the beauty of the countryside.

Camden

- ★ **Tennessee River Freshwater Pearl Museum:** Freshwater pearls are an important part of Tennessee's economy. On a guided tour of this museum, you can see how mussels are farmed and pearls are harvested from them.

WRITING PROJECTS

Check out these ideas for creating a campaign brochure and writing you-are-there narratives. Or research the lives of famous people from Tennessee.

118

ART PROJECTS

You can illustrate the state song, create a dazzling PowerPoint presentation, or learn about the state quarter and design your own.

119

TIMELINE

What happened when? This timeline highlights important events in the state's history—and shows what was happening throughout the United States at the same time.

122

GLOSSARY

Remember the Words to Know from the chapters in this book? They're all collected here.

125

FAST FACTS

Use this section to find fascinating facts about state symbols, land area and population statistics, weather, sports teams, and much more.

126

SCIENCE, TECHNOLOGY, & MATH PROJECTS

Make weather maps, graph population statistics, and research endangered species that live in the state.

120

PRIMARY VS. SECONDARY SOURCES

121

So what are primary and secondary sources? And what's the diff? This section explains all that and where you can find them.

133

BIOGRAPHICAL DICTIONARY

This at-a-glance guide highlights some of the state's most important and influential people. Visit this section and read about their contributions to the state, the country, and the world.

RESOURCES

Books, Web sites, DVDs, and more. Take a look at these additional sources for information about the state.

137

WRITING PROJECTS

★ ★ ★

Write a Memoir, Journal, or Editorial for Your School Newspaper!

Picture Yourself . . .

★ Living in a Cherokee village. Where would you gather food? How would you help build shelter for yourself and your family?

SEE: Chapter Two, pages 32–33.

GO TO: http://tennesseeencyclopedia.net/imagegallery.php?EntryID=O020

★ Taking part in the civil rights movement. Write an editorial for your school newspaper describing your efforts to desegregate Nashville restaurants. Explain how you planned the protest and why you are willing to risk arrest.

SEE: Chapter Five, pages 64–67.

GO TO: http://tennesseeencyclopedia.net/imagegallery.php?EntryID=S043

Create an Election Brochure or Web Site!

Run for office! Throughout this book, you've read about some of the issues that concern Tennessee today. As a candidate for governor of Tennessee, create a campaign brochure or Web site.

★ Explain how you meet the qualifications to be governor of Tennessee.

★ Talk about the three or four major issues you'll focus on if you're elected.

★ Remember, you'll be responsible for Tennessee's budget. How would you spend the taxpayers' money?

SEE: Chapter Seven, pages 87–89.

GO TO: Tennessee's government Web site at www.tennesseeanytime.org. You might also want to read some local newspapers. Try these:

Tennessean (Nashville) at www.tennessean.com

Memphis Daily News at www.memphisdailynews.com

Create an interview script with a famous person from Tennessee!

★ Research various Tennesseans, such as Al Gore, David Crockett, Sequoyah, Ida B. Wells-Barnett, Bessie Smith, Nikki Giovanni, Miley Cyrus, Pat Summitt, or Justin Timberlake.

★ Based on your research, pick one person you would most like to talk with.

★ Write a script of the interview. What questions would you ask? How would this person answer? Create a question-and-answer format. You may want to supplement this writing project with a voice-recording dramatization of the interview.

SEE: Chapters One, Three, Four, Five, and Six, pages 17, 41, 47, 56, 77, 82, and the Biographical Dictionary, pages 133–136.

ART PROJECTS

★ ★ ★

Create a PowerPoint Presentation or Visitors' Guide

Welcome to Tennessee!

Tennessee is a great place to visit and to live! From its natural beauty to its historical sites, there's plenty to see and do. In your PowerPoint presentation or brochure, highlight 10 to 15 of Tennessee's fascinating landmarks. Be sure to include:

★ a map of the state showing where these sites are located

★ photos, illustrations, Web links, natural history facts, geographic stats, climate and weather, plants and wildlife, and recent discoveries

SEE: Chapter Nine, pages 106–115, and Fast Facts, pages126–127.

GO TO: The official tourism Web site for Tennessee at www.tnvacation.com. Download and print maps, photos, and vacation ideas for tourists.

Illustrate the Lyrics to One of the Tennessee State Songs

("My Homeland, Tennessee")

Use markers, paints, photos, collages, colored pencils, or computer graphics to illustrate the lyrics to "My Homeland, Tennessee." Turn your illustrations into a picture book, or scan them into PowerPoint and add music.

SEE: The lyrics to "My Homeland, Tennessee" on page 128.

GO TO: The Tennessee state government Web site at www.tennesseeanytime.org to find out more about the origin of the state song.

State Quarter Project

From 1999 to 2008, the U.S. Mint introduced new quarters commemorating each of the 50 states in the order that they were admitted to the Union. Each state's quarter features a unique design on its back, or reverse.

GO TO: www.usmint.gov/kids and find out what's featured on the back of the Tennessee quarter.

★ Research the significance of the image. Who designed the quarter? Who chose the final design?

★ Design your own Tennessee quarter. What images would you choose for the reverse?

★ Make a poster showing the Tennessee quarter and label each image.

SCIENCE, TECHNOLOGY, & MATH PROJECTS

★ ★ ★

Graph Population Statistics!

★ Compare population statistics (such as ethnic background, birth, death, and literacy rates) in Tennessee counties or major cities.

★ In your graph or chart, look at population density and write sentences describing what the population statistics show; graph one set of population statistics and write a paragraph explaining what the graphs reveal.

SEE: Chapter Six, pages 70–72.

GO TO: The official Web site for the U.S. Census Bureau at www.census.gov and at http://quickfacts.census.gov/qfd/states/04700.html to find out more about population statistics, how they work, and what the statistics are for Tennessee.

Create a Weather Map of Tennessee!

Use your knowledge of Tennessee's geography to research and identify conditions that result in specific weather events. What is it about the geography of Tennessee that makes it vulnerable to things like ice storms? Create a weather map or poster that shows the weather patterns over the state. Include a caption explaining the technology used to measure weather phenomena and provide data.

SEE: Chapter One, pages 17–18.

GO TO: The National Oceanic and Atmospheric Administration's National Weather Service Web site at www.weather.gov for weather maps and forecasts for Tennessee.

Least tern

Track Endangered Species

Using your knowledge of Tennessee's wildlife, research which animals and plants are endangered or threatened.

★ Find out what the state is doing to protect these species.

★ Chart known populations of the animals and plants, and report on changes in certain geographic areas.

SEE: Chapter One, page 19.

GO TO: Web sites such as www.endangeredspecie.com/states/tn.htm for lists of endangered species in Tennessee.

PRIMARY VS. SECONDARY SOURCES

★ ★ ★

What's the Diff?

Your teacher may require at least one or two primary sources and one or two secondary sources for your assignment. So, what's the difference between the two?

★ **Primary sources are original.** You are reading the actual words of someone's diary, journal, letter, autobiography, or interview. Primary sources can also be photographs, maps, prints, cartoons, news/film footage, posters, first-person newspaper articles, drawings, musical scores, and recordings. By the way, when you conduct a survey, interview someone, shoot a video, or take photographs to include in a project, you are creating primary sources!

★ **Secondary sources are what you find in encyclopedias, textbooks, articles, biographies, and almanacs.** These are written by a person or group of people who tell about something that happened to someone else. Secondary sources also recount what another person said or did. This book is an example of a secondary source.

Now that you know what primary sources are—where can you find them?

★ **Your school or local library:** Check the library catalog for collections of original writings, government documents, musical scores, and so on. Some of this material may be stored on microfilm. The Library of Congress Web site (www.loc.gov) is an excellent online resource for primary source materials.

★ **Historical societies:** These organizations keep historical documents, photographs, and other materials. Staff members can help you find what you are looking for. History museums are also great places to see primary sources firsthand.

★ **The Internet:** There are lots of sites that have primary sources you can download and use in a project or assignment.

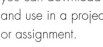

TIMELINE

★ ★ ★

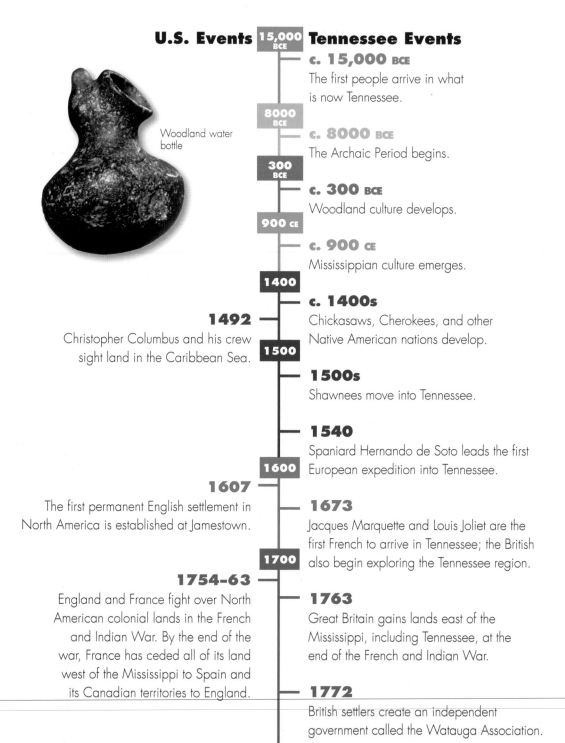

Woodland water bottle

U.S. Events   **15,000 BCE**   **Tennessee Events**

c. 15,000 BCE
The first people arrive in what is now Tennessee.

8000 BCE

c. 8000 BCE
The Archaic Period begins.

300 BCE

c. 300 BCE
Woodland culture develops.

900 CE

c. 900 CE
Mississippian culture emerges.

1400

c. 1400s
Chickasaws, Cherokees, and other Native American nations develop.

1492
Christopher Columbus and his crew sight land in the Caribbean Sea.

1500

1500s
Shawnees move into Tennessee.

1540
Spaniard Hernando de Soto leads the first European expedition into Tennessee.

1600

1607
The first permanent English settlement in North America is established at Jamestown.

1673
Jacques Marquette and Louis Joliet are the first French to arrive in Tennessee; the British also begin exploring the Tennessee region.

1700

1754–63
England and France fight over North American colonial lands in the French and Indian War. By the end of the war, France has ceded all of its land west of the Mississippi to Spain and its Canadian territories to England.

1763
Great Britain gains lands east of the Mississippi, including Tennessee, at the end of the French and Indian War.

1772
British settlers create an independent government called the Watauga Association.

U.S. Events

1776
Thirteen American colonies declare their independence from Great Britain.

1787
The U.S. Constitution is written.

1812–15
The United States and Great Britain fight the War of 1812.

Trail of Tears

1861–65
The American Civil War is fought between the Northern Union and the Southern Confederacy; it ends with the surrender of the Confederate army, led by General Robert E. Lee.

1866
The U.S. Congress approves the Fourteenth Amendment to the U.S. Constitution, granting citizenship to African Americans.

1917–18
The United States engages in World War I.

Tennessee Events

1783
The American Revolution ends, and Tennessee is part of a new nation.

1796
Tennessee becomes the 16th state.

1800

1813
White Americans and Creeks clash in the Creek War.

1815
Tennessean Andrew Jackson becomes a hero in the War of 1812.

1838
Cherokees are forced west on the Trail of Tears.

1861
The Civil War begins, and Tennessee joins the Confederacy.

1866
Tennessee is readmitted to the Union.

Late 1800s
Tennessee enacts Jim Crow laws, establishing legal segregation.

1900

1915
Boll weevils destroy Tennessee's cotton crop.

1916
Millions of African Americans begin moving north in the Great Migration.

124

U.S. Events

1929

The stock market crashes, plunging the United States more deeply into the Great Depression.

1941-45

The United States engages in World War II.

1951-53

The United States engages in the Korean War.

1964-73

The United States engages in the Vietnam War.

Dolly Parton

1991

The United States and other nations engage in the brief Persian Gulf War against Iraq.

2001

Terrorists attack the United States on September 11.

2003

The United States and coalition forces invade Iraq.

2008

The United States elects its first African American president, Barack Obama.

Tennessee Events

1925

John Scopes is tried for teaching evolution in his school.

John Scopes

1955

A court orders Nashville schools to desegregate in the case of *Kelly v. Board of Education*.

1960

Students in Nashville desegregate lunch counters.

1968

Martin Luther King Jr. is assassinated in Memphis.

1980s

Tennessee becomes a center of automobile manufacturing.

1986

Dolly Parton buys a small tourist attraction and turns it into Dollywood.

2000

2007

Tennessee's Al Gore wins the Nobel Peace Prize.

Al Gore

GLOSSARY

abolitionist a person who works to end slavery

appeals legal proceedings in which a court is asked to change the decision of a lower court

breechcloths garments worn by men over their lower bodies

civil rights basic rights that are guaranteed to all people under the U.S. Constitution

Creoles people of French ancestry who lived in the southern United States and spoke a version of French

desegregate to end the practice of keeping races separate from each other in education or other community activities

discrimination unequal treatment based on race, gender, religion, or other factors

emancipator a person who frees someone from slavery or some other form of control

endangered at risk of becoming extinct throughout all or part of its range

erosion the gradual wearing away of rock or soil by physical breakdown, chemical solution, or water

expedition a trip for the purpose of exploration

fast to go without eating

geographers people who study and describe the earth's surface

global warming an increase in temperatures around the globe, particularly as a result of pollution

hydrocarbons chemical compounds made of hydrogen and carbon

hydroelectric plants factories that use water power, typically through a dam, to produce electricity

immunity a body's defense against disease

levees human-made wall-like embankments, often made of earth, built along a river to control flooding

militia an army made up of citizens trained to serve as soldiers in an emergency

missionary a person who tries to convert others to a religion

precipitation all water that falls to the earth, including rain, sleet, hail, snow, dew, fog, or mist

ratified formally approved something, such as a legal document

reservoirs artificial lakes or tanks created for water storage

seceding withdrawing from a group or an organization

sedimentary formed from clay, sand, and gravel that settle at the bottom of a body of water

segregation separation from others, according to race, class, ethnic group, religion, or other factors

suffrage the right to vote

threatened likely to become endangered in the foreseeable future

tributary a smaller river that flows into a larger river

FAST FACTS

State Symbols

State seal

Statehood date June 1, 1796; 16th state
Origin of state name Tanasi was the name of a Cherokee village on the Tennessee River
State capital Nashville
State nickname Volunteer State
State motto "Agriculture and Commerce"
State bird Mockingbird
State game bird Bobwhite quail
State flower Iris
State fish Largemouth bass and channel catfish
State mammal Raccoon
State reptile Eastern box turtle
State amphibian Tennessee cave salamander
State insects Firefly and honeybee
State gem Tennessee river pearl
State rocks Limestone and agate
State mineral Bowenite
State songs "My Homeland, Tennessee," "When It's Iris Time in Tennessee," "The Tennessee Waltz," "My Tennessee," and "Rocky Top"
State public school song "My Tennessee"
State tree Tulip poplar
State bicentennial tree Yellowwood tree
State fossil *Pterotrigonia thoracica*
State fair September in Nashville

Geography

Total area; rank 42,143 square miles (109,150 sq km); 36th
Land; rank 41,217 square miles (106,752 sq km); 34th
Water; rank 926 square miles (2,398 sq km); 32nd
Inland water; rank 926 square miles (2,398 sq km); 24th
Geographic center Rutherford County, 5 miles (8 km) northeast of Murfreesboro
Latitude 35° N to 36°41' N

Longitude 81°37' W to 90°28' W
Highest point Clingmans Dome, 6,643 feet (2,025 m),
located in Sevier County
Lowest point Mississippi River in Shelby County, 178 feet (54 m)
Largest city Memphis
Longest river Tennessee
Number of counties 95

Population

Population; rank (2007 estimate) 6,156,719; 17th
Density (2007 estimate) 149 persons per square mile (58 per sq km)
Population distribution (2000 census) 64% urban, 36% rural
Race (2007 estimate) White persons: 80.4%*

Black persons: 16.9%*
Asian persons: 1.3%*
American Indian and Alaska Native persons: 0.3%*
Native Hawaiian and Other Pacific Islanders: 0.05%*
Persons reporting two or more races: 1.1%
Persons of Hispanic or Latino origin: 3.5%†
White persons not Hispanic: 77.2%

Includes persons reporting only one race.
† Hispanics may be of any race, so they are also included in applicable race categories.

Weather

Record high temperature 113°F (45°C) at Perryville on July 29
and August 9, 1930
Record low temperature −32°F (−36°C) at Mountain City on December 30, 1917
Average July temperature 79°F (26°C)
Average January temperature 37°F (3°C)
Average annual precipitation 48 inches (122 cm)

State flag

STATE SONG

★ ★ ★

"My Homeland, Tennessee"

Tennessee has five official state songs. The oldest of these is "My Homeland, Tennessee," with words by Nell Grayson Taylor and music by Roy Lamont Smith. It became an official state song in 1925.

O Tennessee, that gave us birth,
To thee our hearts bow down.
For thee our love and loyalty
Shall weave a fadeless crown.
Thy purple hills our cradle was;
Thy fields our mother breast;
Beneath thy sunny bended skies
Our childhood days were blessed.

Chorus:
O Tennessee, fair Tennessee,
Our love for thee can never die:
Dear homeland, Tennessee.
'Twas long ago our fathers came,
A free and noble band,
Across the mountains' frowning heights
To seek a promised land.
And here before their raptured eyes,
In beauteous majesty:
Outspread the smiling valleys
Of the winding Tennessee.
Could we forget our heritage
Of heroes strong and brave?
Could we do aught but cherish it,
Unsullied to the grave?
Ah no! The state where Jackson sleeps
Shall ever peerless be.
We glory in thy majesty;
Our homeland, Tennessee!

NATURAL AREAS AND HISTORIC SITES

★ ★ ★

National Historic Site
The *Andrew Johnson National Historic Site* honors the nation's 17th president.

National Park
Great Smoky Mountains National Park is known for its diverse plants and rich history.

National River and Recreation Area
Big South Fork National River and Recreation Area, with its 90 miles (145 km) of scenic gorges and valleys, is a great place to kayak, canoe, fish, horseback ride, mountain bike, or hike.

National Scenic Trail
Tennessee is home to more than 290 miles (467 km) of the 2,174-mile (3,499 km) *Appalachian National Scenic Trail* and boasts the mountain range's highest point.

National Historic Trails
Two national historic trails run through Tennessee. *Overmountain Victory National Historic Trail* follows the route American Patriots took from Virginia to the Battle of Kings Mountain in South Carolina during the American Revolution. The *Trail of Tears National Historic Trail* follows the path Cherokees took as they were forced to move from their homelands.

National Battlefields
Fort Donelson National Battlefield preserves the site of the North's first major victory of the Civil War.

Stones River National Battlefield commemorates a Civil War battle fought for three winter days.

National Military Park
Shiloh National Military Park is on the site of the first major western battle of the Civil War. It is also home to prehistoric Indian mounds.

Wild and Scenic River
Tennessee's *Obed Wild and Scenic River* features beautiful gorges above rolling waters.

Parkway
The *Natchez Trace Parkway* commemorates a trail through Mississippi, Alabama, and Tennessee.

State Parks
Tennessee's state park system features and maintains 55 state parks and recreation areas, including *Booker T. Washington State Park*, which is named after the African American educator; *Davy Crockett Birthplace State Park*, which commemorates the birthplace of American hero Davy Crockett; and *Standing Stone State Park*.

SPORTS TEAMS

NCAA Teams (Division I)

Austin Peay State University *Governors*
Belmont University *Bruins*
East Tennessee State University *Buccaneers*
Lipscomb University *Bisons*
Middle Tennessee State University *Blue Raiders*
Tennessee State University *Tigers*
Tennessee Tech University *Golden Eagles*
University of Memphis *Tigers*
University of Tennessee–Chattanooga *Moccasins*
University of Tennessee–Knoxville *Volunteers*
University of Tennessee–Martin *Skyhawks*
Vanderbilt University *Commodores*

PROFESSIONAL SPORTS TEAMS

National Basketball Association

Memphis *Grizzlies*

National Football League

Tennessee *Titans*

National Hockey League

Nashville *Predators*

CULTURAL INSTITUTIONS

Libraries

The *State Library and Archives* (Nashville) holds important collections of Tennessee history, literature, and biographies as well as state and federal documents.

The *Vanderbilt University Library* (Nashville) and the *University of Tennessee Library* (Knoxville) both have important academic and scholarly collections.

LeMoyne-Owen College Library (Memphis) and the *Fisk University Library* (Nashville) both contain important African American collections.

Abraham Lincoln Library and Museum (Harrogate) contains important Civil War and Lincoln collections.

Museums

The *Tennessee State Museum* (Nashville) features exhibits on the state's history.

The *Cumberland Science Museum* (Nashville) has a planetarium as well as exhibits on science, natural history, and culture.

The *National Civil Rights Museum* (Memphis) is housed in the former motel where Martin Luther King Jr. was assassinated.

The *Country Music Hall of Fame and Museum* (Nashville) commemorates the rich musical traditions of Nashville.

The *Knoxville Museum of Art* has important folk art collections.

The *Carl Van Vechten Gallery* at Fisk University houses important collections of art by African Americans.

Performing Arts

Tennessee has three major opera companies, four major symphony orchestras, and one major dance company.

Universities and Colleges

In 2006, Tennessee had 22 public and 65 private institutions of higher learning.

★ ANNUAL EVENTS

January–March

Chocolate Fest in Knoxville (January)

Eagle Watch tours at Reelfoot Lake near Tiptonville (January–March)

National Field Trial Championship for bird dogs in Grand Junction (February)

Mule Day in Columbia (March/April)

April–June

Dogwood Arts Festival in Knoxville (April)

Spring Wildflower Pilgrimage in Gatlinburg (April)

World's Biggest Fish Fry in Paris (April)

East Tennessee Strawberry Festival in Dayton (May)

Iroquois Steeplechase in Nashville (May)

Festival of British and Appalachian Culture in Rugby (May)

Memphis in May International Festival (May)

West Tennessee Strawberry Festival in Humboldt (May)

International Country Music Fan Fair in Nashville (June)

Riverbend Festival in Chattanooga (June)

Rhododendron Festival in Roan Mountain (June)

Frontier Days in Lynchburg (June)

July–September

Smithville Fiddlers' Jamboree and Crafts Festival (July)

Tennessee Walking Horse National Celebration in Shelbyville (late August/early September)

International Grand Championship Walking Horse Show in Murfreesboro (September)

Agricultural and Industrial Fair in Knoxville (September)

Mid-South Fair in Memphis (September)

Tennessee State Fair in Nashville (September)

October–December

Historic Rugby Pilgrimage of Homes (October)

National Storytelling Festival in Jonesborough (October)

Autumn Gold Festival in Coker Creek (October)

Oktoberfest in Memphis (October)

Fall Color Cruise and Folk Festival in Chattanooga (October)

Tennessee Fall Homecoming at Museum of Appalachia in Clinton (October)

Fall Craftsmen's Fair in Gatlinburg (October)

Smoky Mountain Winterfest in Gatlinburg (November–February)

BIOGRAPHICAL DICTIONARY

Roy C. Acuff (1903–1992), who was born in Maynardville, was often called the King of Country Music. He appeared frequently on the Grand Ole Opry and was the first living artist to be elected to the Country Music Hall of Fame.

Lamar Alexander (1940–), a native of Maryville, is a longtime politician. He has served as Tennessee governor, the U.S. secretary of education, and a U.S. senator.

Chet Atkins (1924–2001), who was born in Luttrell, was one of country music's greatest guitar players. He was also a music producer who worked with artists such as Waylon Jennings, Dolly Parton, Charley Pride, and Willie Nelson.

Attakullakulla See page 39.

Marilou Awiakta (1936–) is a poet and public speaker who links Cherokee history to modern issues. She was born in Oak Ridge.

DeFord Bailey See page 79.

Kathy Bates (1948–), an Academy Award–winning actress, was born and raised in Memphis. She has appeared in films such as *Fried Green Tomatoes* and *The Golden Compass*.

Bill Belichick (1952–), a native of Nashville, is a successful National Football League coach. He became the coach of the New England Patriots in 2000, and by 2004 the team had won three Super Bowls.

Bill Belichick

Mary Frances Berry (1938–) of Nashville is a leading historian and civil rights activist. She served as the vice chair of the U.S. Commission on Civil Rights for two years.

Arna Bontemps (1902–1973) was a writer in the Harlem Renaissance, a flowering of African American culture in New York City in the early 20th century. In 1943, he became head librarian at Fisk University. He later arranged for a collection of resources from his Harlem Renaissance friends to be donated to the school. In 1949, he and Langston Hughes edited *The Poetry of the Negro*. Years later, the pair edited *The Book of Negro Folklore*.

Ralph Boston (1939–) was born in Mississippi and attended Tennessee State University, where he won the national collegiate long jump title. He competed in the 1960, 1964, and 1968 Olympics, winning three medals.

Dorothy L. Brown See page 66.

Kathy Bates

Tracy Caulkins (1963–) attended school in Nashville and went on to win Olympic gold medals in swimming in 1984.

Isabel Cobb (1858–1947), born in Morgantown, was of Cherokee and European descent. In 1870, her family moved to the Cherokee Nation in Indian Territory. She taught high school and then became a doctor. For years, she focused on providing medical care for women and children in their homes in Wagoner, Indian Territory.

David Crockett See page 41.

Miley Cyrus (1992–) is a singer from Nashville who plays the character Hannah Montana on TV. In 2008, she was listed as one of *Time* magazine's 100 Most Influential People in the World among artists and entertainers.

Sam Davis (1842–1863), a native of Rutherford County, fought for the Confederacy during the Civil War. In 1863, he became one of Coleman's Scouts, soldiers who worked behind Union lines to disrupt communications. He was caught in 1863 and found guilty of being a spy. Given one last chance to reveal his source, he refused and was hanged. Right before he was executed, supposedly he said, "Officer, I did my duty. Now, you do yours."

Anne Dallas Dudley See page 61.

Miley Cyrus

Belle Edmondson (1840–1873) grew up in Shelby County. During the Civil War, soldiers and scouts from both sides traveled through her family's farm. As a spy and smuggler for the Confederate army, she often carried letters, money, and medicine hidden in her clothes.

Elihu Embree (1782–1820) was an abolitionist and publisher of the *Emancipator*.

Jane Greenebaum Eskind (1933–) was the first woman in Tennessee to win a statewide election. In 1980, she was elected to a seat on the Public Service Commission.

David G. Farragut (1801–1870), a native of Stoney Point, commanded the USS *Saratoga* during the Mexican War in the late 1840s. He later became an admiral in the Union navy. He is remembered for having said, "Damn the torpedoes! Full speed ahead!"

Cornelia Fort (1919–1943) was born to a wealthy Nashville family but made her name as an airplane pilot. In 1941, she was in Hawai'i when Japanese planes bombed Pearl Harbor. She joined the Women's Auxiliary Ferrying Squadron, flying new planes from factories to military bases. She died in a midair collision in 1943 while ferrying a plane to Texas.

Cornelia Fort

Nikki Giovanni See page 82.

Al Gore See page 17.

Alex Haley (1921–1992) was a writer who spent his childhood in Henning. He is best known for his novel *Roots: The Saga of an American Family*, which tells the story of an African captured by slave traders and how his story was passed down through his descendants. *Roots* was made into a 12-hour TV miniseries in 1977, sparking many Americans' interests in tracing their own roots.

Benjamin Hooks (1925–) is a lawyer, Baptist minister, and civil rights leader. He served as executive director of the National Association for the Advancement of Colored People (NAACP) from 1977 until 1992. He broadened the NAACP's areas of interest, expanding concerns beyond civil rights. He promoted NAACP involvement in the environment, ecology, and energy.

Julia Britton Hooks (1852–1942) was an African American music teacher known as the Angel of Beale Street. She founded the Hooks School of Music in Memphis. She also openly opposed the Jim Crow laws that insisted she sit in the "colored" section of a Memphis theater and was fined $5 for refusing to move from the white section.

Andrew Jackson See page 93.

Alex Haley

Samuel L. Jackson

Samuel L. Jackson (1948–) grew up in Chattanooga and became an actor on the stage and in movies. He has played a wide range of roles, including a Jedi master in *Star Wars: Episode I—The Phantom Menace*.

Andrew Johnson See page 93.

Belle Kinney (1890–1959) was a sculptor from Nashville who worked in bronze. Among her greatest works is *Victory*, which stands in the atrium of the War Memorial Building. She also completed busts of Andrew Jackson and James K. Polk that are in the Tennessee state capitol.

Nanye-hi (Nancy Ward) (c. 1738–1822) of Chota was a Cherokee leader and warrior who was influential in establishing peace between the Cherokees and white settlers.

Dolly Parton See page 99.

Sam Phillips See page 100.

James K. Polk See page 93.

Charley Pride (1938–) is a country music star who had hits such as "Kiss an Angel Good Morning." He was the first African American superstar in country music.

Wilma Rudolph See page 83.

Robert Ryman See page 112.

Sequoyah See page 47.

Bessie Smith See page 77.

Pat Summitt (1952–), a native of Clarksville, is the women's basketball coach at the University of Tennessee–Knoxville. She played on the U.S. women's basketball team that won the silver medal at the 1976 Olympic Games. By that time, she was already coaching the University of Tennessee team. She won the Naismith College Coach of the Year Award three times, and in 2000 she was named the Naismith Coach of the Century. She was elected to the National Basketball Hall of Fame in 2000.

Justin Timberlake (1981–), who was born in Memphis, is a dancer, singer, songwriter, record producer, and actor. He has won six Grammy Awards for his music. Once a part of the group 'N Sync, he has performed at the Olympics, the Academy Awards, and the Super Bowl.

Justin Timberlake

Tina Turner (1939–) is a rock and soul singer whose energy is legendary. She has sold more than 100 million albums and has had many hit songs, including "Proud Mary," "River Deep, Mountain High," and "What's Love Got to Do with It." She was born in Nutbush.

Tina Turner

Usher (1978–) is an award-winning rhythm-and-blues and hip-hop singer who grew up in Chattanooga. His hits include "Yeah!" and "Burn."

Robert Penn Warren (1905–1989) was a poet and novelist whose work often reflected southern themes. His novel *All the King's Men*, about a charismatic Louisiana governor, won the Pulitzer Prize for Fiction in 1947. Warren also won the Pulitzer Prize for Poetry two times.

Ida B. Wells-Barnett See page 56.

Reese Witherspoon (1976–) is a popular actress who was raised in Nashville. She won an Academy Award for *Walk the Line*. She has also appeared in hits such as *Legally Blonde* and *Pleasantville*.

Alvin C. York (1887–1964), a native of Pall Mall, was one of the great heroes of World War I. In 1918, he saved the lives of some of his fellow soldiers and captured 132 enemy prisoners. His story is told in the 1941 movie *Sergeant York*.

RESOURCES

BOOKS

Nonfiction

Arnold, James R., and Roberta Wiener. *River to Victory: The Civil War in the West, 1861–1863*. Minneapolis: Lerner Publications, 2002.

De Capua, Sarah. *The Wilderness Road*. Mankato, Minn.: Compass Point Books, 2006.

Hawkes, Steve. *The Tennessee River*. Milwaukee: Gareth Stevens, 2003.

Marsh, Carole. *Tennessee Indians*. Peachtree City, Ga.: Gallopade International, 2004.

McClellan, Adam. *Uniquely Tennessee*. Chicago: Heinemann Library, 2004.

Watkins, Samuel R. *The Diary of Sam Watkins, a Confederate Soldier*. Tarrytown, N.Y.: Benchmark Books, 2003.

Fiction

Barrett, Tracy. *Cold in Summer*. New York: Henry Holt and Company, 2003.

Crist-Evans, Craig. *Moon over Tennessee: A Boy's Civil War Journal*. Boston: Houghton Mifflin, 2003.

Hermes, Patricia. *Sweet By and By*. New York: HarperCollins, 2002.

Partridge, Elizabeth. *Clara and the Hoodoo Man*. New York: Puffin Books, 1998.

Steele, William O. *Flaming Arrows*. New York: Odyssey Classics, 2004.

Wisler, G. Clifton. *Thunder on the Tennessee*. New York: Puffin Books, 1995.

DVDs

The Color of Autumn: Fall in the Great Smoky Mountains. CustomFlix, 2007.

Discoveries . . . America: Tennessee. Bennett-Watt Entertainment, 2005.

Grand Ole Opry Video Collection: The Hall of Fame. Time Life, 2007.

Sergeant York. Warner Home Video, 2006.

This Is Elvis. Warner Home Video, 2007.

WEB SITES AND ORGANIZATIONS

The American Civil War Homepage
http://sunsite.utk.edu/civil-war/warweb.html
To find out more about Tennessee during the Civil War.

Grand Ole Opry
www.opry.com
This site provides a schedule of events and information about country-and-western musicians.

Great Smoky Mountains National Park
www.nps.gov/grsm
For great information about the national park.

National Civil Rights Museum
www.civilrightsmuseum.org/home.htm
Learn about exhibits and find out what's happening at the museum that honors the history of civil rights.

Tennessee Encyclopedia of History and Culture
http://tennesseeencyclopedia.net
To find out about Tennessee's history and culture and to read biographies of Tennesseans.

Tennessee Government
www.state.tn.us
The official Tennessee Web site has all kinds of information about the state government along with information for tourists.

Tennessee Vacation
www.tnvacation.com
Check out vacation ideas and find fun things to do in the Volunteer State.

INDEX

★ ★ ★

AUTHOR'S TIPS AND SOURCE NOTES

★ ★ ★

Researching this book required many trips to the library, a tour through Amazon.com, and endless hours searching the Internet. *The Tennessee Encyclopedia of History and Culture* at http://tennesseeencyclopedia.net had a wide range of information. Among the most useful books I read were *Tennessee History: The Land, the People, and the Culture*, which was edited by Carroll Van West, and *The Civil War in Tennessee, 1862–1863,* by Jack H. Lepa.